EMT CAREER STARTER

EMT
career starter

2nd edition

Cheryl Hancock
with Lauren B. Starkey

LEARNINGEXPRESS

New York

Library of Congress Cataloging-in-Publication Data:
Hancock, Cheryl.
    EMT career starter / Cheryl Hancock with Lauren B. Starkey—2nd ed.
      p. cm.
    Earlier ed. published with subtitle: Finding and getting a great job.
    Includes bibliographical references.
    ISBN 1-57685-366-7 (pbk.)
    1. Emergency medical technicians—Vocational guidance.   I. Starkey, Lauren B.,
  1962– II. Title.

RA645.5 .H36 2001
616.02'5'023—dc21   00-053479

Printed in the United States of America
9 8 7 6 5 4 3 2 1
Second Edition

Regarding the Information in this Book

Every effort has been made to ensure the accuracy of directory information up until press time. However, phone numbers and/or addresses are subject to change. Please contact the respective organization for the most recent information.

For Further Information

For information on LearningExpress, other LearningExpress products, or bulk sales, please write to us at:

    LearningExpress™
    900 Broadway
    Suite 604
    New York, NY 10003

Or visit our website at:
  www.learnatest.com

Contents

Contents

Introduction

EMTs, or Emergency Medical Technicians, and paramedics are employed in a number of industries. About two-fifths work for local and suburban private ambulance firms that transport and treat individuals on an emergency or non-emergency basis. About a third of the EMTs and paramedics work for local fire departments and third-service providers, independent agencies, that provide emergency medical services. Another fourth work for hospitals, where they may work full-time within the medical facility or respond to calls in ambulances or helicopters to transport critically ill or injured patients.

The Bureau of Labor Statistics reports that there were about 150,000 paid full-time EMTs working in the United States in 1998. That number doesn't include the many volunteer EMTs working in smaller cities, towns, and rural areas. It is projected that the need for more EMTs will grow at a rate higher than that for most other professions through 2008. In fact, during the decade 1996–2006, a 45% increase in the number of EMTs employed is expected. But just because the emergency medical services field requires a larger labor force, don't expect to sail into your first job without working hard to attain it.

There is stiff competition for EMT positions, especially those in larger companies, where salaries are higher and the opportunities for advancement greater. Not only will you have to have the proper training for your future career, but you'll also have to pass state and/or national exams to receive certification as either an EMT-Basic, EMT-Intermediate, or EMT-Paramedic. Some employers also require advanced certification or training. You'll be working in the medical field, in which advances in treatment and technology occur all the time. In order to perform your job at an optimal level, you will need to keep up with those advances as they pertain to emergency medical services.

You can increase your chances of landing a job in prehospital care by reading this book and applying what you've learned to your job search. Not only will you learn about the various training courses available, but you'll also learn how to find them and how to pay for them. Other subjects covered include the complicated job application process, the different types of jobs available in the field, and how to succeed once you've landed a job. Throughout the book, you will find helpful information from those already working in emergency medical services, in both the quick tips found within the chapters and the more in-depth interviews found at the end of each chapter.

Chapter 1 gives an overview of the emergency medical services (EMS) field. You'll learn about the rewards and responsibilities of the job as well as the certification process. This chapter also explains the best opportunities in prehospital care today; full-time, part-time, and volunteer positions are discussed, as well as the many different employers of EMTs. Finally, you can take an evaluation at the end of the chapter to help determine whether work as an EMT is for you.

Chapter 2 is all about training programs: how to evaluate them and how to choose the right one for you. You'll find out about entrance requirements, and you'll be given some key questions to ask about the training program you're interested in. You will also find sample course descriptions. An extensive directory of schools that offer basic, intermediate, and paramedic EMT courses is included as an appendix.

Once you've decided on the training you want and need, Chapter 3 will help you find the money to pay for it. The three types of financial aid (scholarships and grants, loans, and work-study programs) are explained. You'll find out how to determine your eligibility for each, which financial records you'll need to gather, and how to complete and file forms (a sample financial aid form is included). At the end of the chapter are listed many more resources that can help you find the aid you need.

In Chapter 4, you'll learn about the job search process, from discovering who's hiring to getting through the application process. We'll take you step by step from writing query letters and resumes to the interview background check. Many sample documents, such as applications and resumes, are included. To ensure your success with a job search, a variety of insider tips from current EMTs are added.

Finally, after you've been hired, Chapter 5 will show how you can best succeed on the job. You'll find out how to become a top performer in emergency medical services, learning the qualities that are rewarded, the procedures for moving up in the ranks, and the best ways to interact with coworkers and supervisors. Thinking ahead, we'll cover the promotion process and some of the many alternative careers that are open to experienced EMTs.

Good luck with your job search and new career!

EMT CAREER STARTER

CHAPTER one

CHOOSING TO WORK AS AN EMT

IN THIS chapter, you'll gain an overview of the emergency medical services, or EMS, field. You'll learn about hiring trends, the many rewards of the job, and the working conditions of EMTs. Then read a current report from the field on the best opportunities in prehospital care today, from working for a private or a hospital ambulance service to municipal employment with a fire or police department. Full-time, part-time, and volunteer positions are discussed, as are the differences between the titles EMT-Basic, EMT-Intermediate, and EMT-Paramedic and the certification procedures required for each. Finally, you'll be able to use an evaluation at the end of the chapter to help you determine whether work as an EMT is right for you.

IF YOU'VE ever been involved in an accident or other crisis situation, you may have been in need of prehospital care. If you were helped by an EMT, you know how important the work of this emergency specialist is. EMTs aid and save millions of lives each year.

EMTs respond to medical emergencies, especially 911 calls, to provide immediate treatment for sick or injured persons both on the scene of an accident and during ambulance transport to a medical facility. There are half a million practicing EMTs in the United States today. These technicians are the first care providers to arrive at the scene of an accident, and their adequate assessment of treatment is crucial to the life of the victim. They function as part of an emergency medical team, and the range of medical and lifesaving services they perform varies according to their level of training.

Many people decide to become EMTs knowing how they may help another in a crisis situation. Some become EMTs after having been rescued by technicians. Theresa Sims, an EMT-Intermediate from Wilmington, Delaware, explains:

I became an EMT after having been rescued by one. I was riding too fast on my bicycle on a bicycle path on a resort island, trying to beat a storm that was coming. As I rounded a corner that was sheltered by some bushes, I suddenly saw a couple on bikes heading toward me too quickly to stop. I turned toward the grass when the woman's bike hit head-on into the side of my bike, and at the same time, her forehead hit me behind my left ear. The pain I felt was unbearable, like my head was splitting open. Luckily, someone went to the hotel across the street and dialed 911. The ambulance came, and the EMTs realized how badly I could've been hurt. I spent about 20 minutes with that team trying to keep me awake and talking to me, and then, when the local hospital didn't have a neurologist, I spent an hour with another team being transported to the next major city. I had a skull fracture and a subdural hematoma [blood clot below the skull], and from what they told me, I could've died. The time I spent with the EMTs made me think about what might have happened to me if they had not come to help me or to transport me to someone who could. That's when I decided I could return the favor to someone else someday, that EMTs must receive enormous satisfaction from helping those in need.

HIRING TRENDS

According to the Bureau of Labor Statistics, the total number of jobs for EMTs is expected to grow faster than the average of all occupations through 2008. By 2006, there should be a 45% increase in the number of EMTs and paramedics employed since 1996. But this growth is not expected to occur evenly throughout the United States; some areas will likely see more, while others will see much less.

One important factor affecting hiring trends is the aging population; as the average age of Americans increases, the need for emergency medical services will also grow. Another factor follows from the first; in order to serve a larger older population, states are building more fire stations and hospitals and beginning to allow certified EMT-Paramedics to perform primary care on the scene, without transporting the patient to a medical facility.

Many communities understand the importance of high-quality emergency medical services and are willing and able to raise tax dollars to support them. In these often larger communities, the employment outlook should remain favorable. Volunteer services are being phased out in these areas, and well-equipped emergency services operated by salaried EMTs are replacing them. However, in some communities, particularly smaller ones, the employment outlook is not as favorable.

Maintaining a high-quality EMS delivery system can be expensive, and financial strains on local governments could hinder the growth of these services. In addition, cutbacks in federal aid to local communities and an overall national effort to harness medical spending may lead to reducing community-based health-related costs. Under these conditions, such communities may not be able to afford the level of emergency medical services that they would otherwise like to provide, and the employment prospects here may be limited to volunteers.

JUST THE FACTS

THE STAR OF LIFE

Each arm of the Star of Life, the official symbol of EMS workers, represents one EMS function:

1. detection
2. reporting
3. response
4. on-scene care
5. care in transit
6. transfer to definitive care

The snake and staff are an ancient Greek symbol of medicine taken from the legend of Aesculapius, the Greek god of healing.

The Star of Life was designed in 1973 by Leo R. Schwartz, EMS branch chief at the National Highway Traffic Safety Administration (NHTSA), to be used by U.S. emergency medical services after the American Red Cross objected to the unauthorized use of its symbol.

JOB RESPONSIBILITIES

The goals of emergency medical technicians are to quickly identify the nature of the emergency, stabilize the patient's condition, and begin the proper procedures to help the victim at the scene and en route to a hospital. EMTs are sent out to emergencies in an ambulance by a dispatcher. The dispatcher acts as a communications channel and may also be trained as an EMT.

EMTs are often the first qualified aid-giving personnel to arrive at an emergency scene, so they must make the initial evaluation of the nature and extent of the victim's medical problem. The accuracy of this early assessment is crucial to the victim's recovery. The duties and capabilities of an emergency medical technician depend mostly on the amount of training he or she received. However, all EMTs are trained and qualified to:

▶ give cardiopulmonary resuscitation (CPR) to a person suffering cardiac arrest
▶ control the bleeding of a victim
▶ administer oxygen to someone who has stopped breathing
▶ deliver babies
▶ subdue a person's violent behavior
▶ treat allergic reactions
▶ apply splints and antishock suits
▶ treat wounds

Once on the scene, EMTs must be quick thinkers and cope immediately and effectively with whatever situation is awaiting them. They must be on the lookout for any clues such as medical identification emblems indicating that a victim has significant allergies, diabetes, a heart problem, epilepsy, or other conditions that might affect decisions about emergency treatment. Because people who have been involved with an emergency are sometimes very upset, EMTs must also work with both victims and bystanders in a reassuring manner. They need to know what questions to ask bystanders or family members when more information is needed about a patient.

EMT-Intermediate Gary Anderson from Phoenix, Arizona, describes the qualities an EMT should have to respond appropriately to an accident:

An EMT must be a people person. By that I mean someone who cares for people, their feelings, and their struggle within an emergency situation. An EMT should also have a friendly and team-guided personality to be able to work with other EMTs or fire or police personnel on the scene. EMTs should be emotionally stable, levelheaded, have good flexibility, agility, and physical coordination, and be able to lift and carry heavy loads. EMTs who work as firefighters must be physically fit to get victims out of dangerous situations such as wrecked cars or burning buildings. They also need good eyesight, especially when driving an ambulance at night.

EMTs who drive ambulances must be able to get to and from an emergency scene in any part of their community quickly and safely. Drivers learn these skills in required ambulance training courses. Many EMTs work in two-person teams: one drives while the other monitors the patient's vital signs and gives whatever care is needed. For the protection of the public and themselves, EMT drivers must obey the traffic laws that apply to emergency vehicles. They must be familiar with the roads and any special conditions affecting the choice of route, such as traffic, weather-related problems, and road construction. When preparing to transport patients to a medical facility, EMTs may use special equipment such as backboards to immobilize them before placing them on stretchers and securing them in the ambulance.

The choice of hospital or medical facility is not always decided by EMTs, but when it is, they must base the decision on their knowledge of the equipment and staffing needed by the patient(s). The receiving hospital's emergency department must be informed by radio, either directly or through the dispatcher, of details such as the number of people being transported and the nature of any medical problems. EMTs continue to monitor the patient(s) and administer care as directed by the medical professionals with whom they are maintaining radio contact. When necessary, EMTs also try to be sure that contact has been initiated with any utility companies, municipal repair crews, or other services that should be called to correct dangerous problems, such as fallen power lines or tree limbs, at the emergency scene.

Once at the hospital or medical facility, EMTs help the staff bring the victim(s) into the emergency department and may assist with the first steps of in-hospital care. They supply whatever information they can about each victim's situation, verbally and in writing, for the hospital's records. In the case of a victim's death, the EMTs complete the necessary procedures to ensure that the deceased's property is protected. Bill Boyd, paramedic and fire captain, explains caring for patient belongings:

> We carry patient belonging bags on our medic units. If we note something really expensive, we try to give it to a relative on the scene or take it to the hospital with us and turn it over to the hospital personnel. What we consider valuable may not necessarily be what the patient considers important. Dentures are one of the most common items misplaced, and they are not cheap to replace!

Once a patient has been delivered to the hospital, the EMTs must check in with their dispatchers and then return to their EMS site to prepare the vehicle for another emergency call. This includes replacing used linens and blankets and replenishing drug supplies, oxygen, and other equipment. The EMTs also need to send out equipment to be sterilized and take inventory of the contents of the ambulance to assure completeness. At least once during the shift, they must also check the gas, oil, battery, siren, brakes, radio, and other systems of the vehicle. It is also imperative that EMTs arrive on time for shift changes, to receive and exchange equipment with coworkers.

EMTs may also have optional instructional duties. Emergency medical service companies provide the public with safety classes, which may consist of as little as one lecture on a specific topic or as much as a four-part CPR course. EMTs can also earn extra income by teaching these types of classes for the American Heart Association and other groups.

THE REWARDS OF WORKING AS AN EMT

There are many benefits to working as an EMT. The satisfaction of providing a necessary public service and helping those in need, the excitement of each call being different from the one before, and the steady employment with medical benefits and paid vacations are all on the list.

Personal Benefits

On a daily basis, EMTs care for people. They literally come to the rescue, and they save countless lives. An EMT describes the personal satisfaction of the job:

> After having watched a child wait 45 minutes for an emergency team to come to the scene where she had been hit by a car, about 10 others and I decided that we could provide the service better. Of course, that was a time when EMS services were rare. Now I am a part of our local ambulance/fire service which includes three ambulances, two fire trucks, and a staff of 20 paid EMTs and 10 volunteer EMTs. The waiting period for a call in our town now is less than two minutes.

Peter Herslow, president of the Chatham, New Jersey, Emergency Squad, explains that not only is it rewarding to help others, but the career offers exciting challenges as well. He personally finds getting a call to a large accident scene gratifying, as it requires his best management skills.

Work Environment

Many EMTs describe the work environment as a benefit. The intensity of the job often brings a closeness and camaraderie among those who work together that can't be experienced by those who work in calmer environments. Volunteer EMT Gwen Gray from the Knightdale Emergency Medical Service in North Carolina explains:

> We have paramedics provided by the county who are at the squads on a two-month rotating basis. I really enjoy meeting the different people who come through Knightdale. I have made some great friendships, enjoyed some fabulous gourmet meals, gotten new insight into other professions, and just had a wonderful time laughing with some of the best people in the world. I would trust them with my life (literally!). It's like having a second family you can depend on when you need them!

Many people are drawn to the EMT field because they do not want to sit behind a desk for 40 hours a week. While work schedules vary, they almost always differ from the typical nine-to-five, because emergencies occur around the clock.

Entrance into the Health Care Field

Becoming an EMT is one way to evaluate your interest in health care. You may find that you enjoy it so much that you decide to return to school to become a registered nurse, physician, or other healthcare worker. Robert Kagel, an assistant EMT chief, describes why he loves being an EMT:

> There is no one particular item concerning EMS that I can pin down that I enjoy the most. I just love it. It is a combination of the adrenaline rush, the element of the unknown, the people, the connection you make, the networking you do, the patients you help, the families you support in their time of need, and so much more. The camaraderie is the best of all. Many people say that they couldn't do my job . . . I think if you have a passion to help, more than likely, you can do my job. I use EMS as an escape. While I am heavily involved with it managerialwise and clinical-wise, there is always an escape in it for me. It is my form of relaxation.

Employer Benefits

EMTs usually have a choice of health plans to select from their employer. These plans normally cover the EMT and his or her dependents. Life and disability insurance may also be provided. In addition, a certain number of paid holidays and vacation days, dental and vision insurance, and pension (retirement) plans are usually also offered by EMT employers. And some companies offer free life insurance and overtime pay for court duty.

A uniform allowance may also be offered, as well as limited equipment allowances. Those EMTs who work for police and fire departments receive the same benefits as firefighters and police officers no matter what their EMT level is.

Many EMTs would describe their salary as a benefit; they are receiving a salary for the opportunity to help others in need. As discussed later in this chapter, the salary EMTs earn depends on the level of training, individual experience, and type of employer. Those working in the public sector, for police and fire departments, usually receive a higher wage than those in the private sector who work for ambulance companies and hospitals.

WORK CONDITIONS

EMTs work in extreme environments, whether they are outdoors in adverse weather conditions or in a victim's home with distressed family members. Regardless of the weather, the strenuous physical aspects of the job, such as lifting, climbing, and kneeling, must be performed properly. EMTs must have the physical stamina and professional skills to be able to handle this aspect of their work.

Emotionally, EMTs must be able to cope well with situations such as deaths, accidents, and serious injuries that many people would find upsetting and traumatic. They work under constant duress, having to use quick thinking skills and solid judgment to aid in critical, traumatic situations. The upside of this difficult work is that EMTs can receive enormous satisfaction from knowing that they are able to provide a vital service to victims of sudden illness or accident. Ernie Paul, an EMT-Intermediate from Pasadena, California, says:

> I really enjoy being able to help others, but sometimes it gets rough. I think there is something definitely wrong with a person if what they see as an EMT at an accident scene does not bother them. Sometimes what I see and have to deal with makes me appreciate life more, and sometimes I wonder what is going on with the world. It takes a lot of dedication to perform emergency services for severe incidents, but it's rewarding, on the other hand, to help someone. They help balance each other. But on occasion, when you know the patient just isn't going to make it, no matter what you do for them, that's when I really have to stop and think about what I'm doing as an EMT.

Some EMTs work on rotating shifts, working a 24-hour shift for one to three days and then having two or three days off. Others work a single shift every day, totaling anywhere from 40 to more than 55 hours a week. Since emergency services are required on a 24-hour basis, night and weekend work is often required, and many technicians are on call for emergencies. Usually they must work irregular hours, including some holidays.

Volunteer EMTs work much shorter hours. A typical schedule would put a volunteer at work one or two nights or days a week and on call the rest of the time. For firefighter-EMTs, the work schedule often consists of 24 hours on duty followed by 48 or even 72 hours off duty. Some firefighter-EMTs use their days off to work outside jobs or conduct other business for side income to supplement their salary.

While on duty, EMTs in less busy departments may have small amounts of free time after the maintenance and training for their shift is finished to visit or eat until the next call comes in. However, many EMTs do not have any downtime, because when they are not going out on emergency calls, they must stock supplies, clean equipment, or undergo training. The level and intensity of the workload for EMTs varies among the companies, locations, and population levels in their territory.

WHO EMPLOYS EMTS?

According to the *Journal of Emergency Medical Services*, about two-fifths of all full-time paid EMTs work for private ambulance services, one-third for municipal, police, or rescue squad departments, and one-fourth for hospitals. EMTs also work in industrial plants and other local organizations that provide prehospital emergency care. Below, these employers are compared and contrasted.

Hospital Ambulance Services

One of the leading employers of EMTs are hospital ambulance services. Those who work for these services perform a number of tasks, ranging from simple transport of hospital patients to responding to 911 calls to the scene of an emergency. Hospital ambulance services transfer many kinds of patients to the hospital, home, or a doctor's office. They also assist with neonatal (baby) teams and cardiac technicians. When not on a call, these EMTs clean and stock ambulance rigs, perform other company duties, and may be called to help in the hospital emergency room. This is a great place to begin work as an EMT-Basic, because the varied routine enables adequate learning of EMT basics.

Private Ambulance Services

These services are not affiliated with hospitals and are usually funded or subsidized by the county, city, or volunteer organization for the community. Private ambulance services perform the same basic duties as hospital services do, such as transporting patients, and they are usually connected to the local area 911 system. In many cases, private services have fewer chores than hospital ambulance services, leaving EMTs with more downtime.

Fire Departments

Fire departments are becoming leading employers of EMTs, as there is a growing national trend toward the merging of emergency services. However, to work in a fire department, an EMT must also be trained as a firefighter. If he or she is the first responder to the scene of an accident, the firefighter-EMTs can give emergency aid and medical attention limited to the equipment carried. Some fire stations have an ambulance; those that don't carry limited medical equipment on the fire truck. Firefighter-EMTs give immediate emergency first aid until further ambulance help arrives.

Police Departments

As with fire departments, many police departments are hiring officers who are also EMTs. These departments equip their police cars with medical equipment, including automatic external defibrillation units (AEDs), so that their certified officers can give essential medical aid if they are first to respond to an accident scene. Working for a police department has many advantages, including relatively early retirement with a lifetime pension (retired officers often begin second careers while collecting their pensions). However, the work is often more dangerous than that of an EMT working for another type of employer.

Industrial Plants

EMTs also work on staff or on call for industrial plants that may or may not be located far away from emergency services. Many times people become victims of the machines they operate, so having an EMT on-site ensures that these victims have immediate emergency care. These EMTs usually have less training and available medical equipment than ambulance EMT workers have, but they can tend to a victim until further help arrives. Advantages to working for an industrial plant include regular hours (unless the plant runs 24 hours a day) and more predictable emergency scenarios.

Air Medical Transport Facilities

Air medical transport facilities require the use of certified EMT-Paramedics. These units transport patients by helicopter and airplane locally, nationally, and internationally. Air medical programs transport numerous pediatric patients, and many fly high-risk maternal patients. They are a growing employer within the emergency medical services field, as demand for medical transport increases each year and is predicted to continue to do so. In addition to many job openings, air medical transport work has the added benefit of travel opportunities.

Other EMT Employers

Other organizations that hire EMTs include ski patrols and search-and-rescue units, which provide emergency services in remote or difficult-to-get-to areas. EMTs can also be found at football games, concerts, parades, fairs, carnivals, amusement parks, and other recreational sites. They may be hired privately by an event organizer or hired from a local ambulance company to do standby with one or two crews.

Last, there are the Armed Forces (Army, Navy, Marines, Air Force, and Coast Guard) and the American Red Cross. To become an EMT within the military, see the section on the Armed Forces later in this chapter. To join the Red Cross, you simply volunteer. You can become a volunteer even if you don't have any training; however, you will not be able to advance without it. There are some paid positions within the Red Cross, but they require certification and training, and in many cases they hire those who have volunteered first.

JOB OPPORTUNITIES FOR EMTS

The most visible EMTs are those who work for ambulance services; however, there are numerous job opportunities for the many different kinds of EMTs. The more education an EMT obtains, the more positions are open to him or her.

Volunteer EMTs

Volunteer EMTs are considered a rare breed of people. They can be found in both fire stations and private ambulance services, most likely in small rural communities. Some choose this work to evaluate their interest in the occupation before looking for a job opening. Others become volunteers because a company requested it as a first step before being hired full-time. As a new volunteer, you may be required to run any call that comes in as a "third person," to gain as much experience as you can. After putting in your time as a rookie, you will then be assigned to work better hours.

Paid EMTs

EMTs with more experience and education can work for a salary. The majority of paid positions exist in larger metropolitan cities such as Atlanta,

Dallas, or Phoenix. There also tend to be more openings in such urban areas because the turnover rate for EMTs is higher there. The most common paid EMT positions include EMT-Basic, EMT-Intermediate, EMT-Paramedic, dispatcher, firefighter, police officer, air transport, and career Armed Forces EMTs.

IN THE NEWS

Tax Breaks for EMTs

New Fairfield, Connecticut, has unanimously voted to give its volunteer firefighters and EMTs a property tax reduction as a way of thanking them for their service and to encourage other citizens to become volunteers. The ordinance passed by the town of 13,000 will take effect in July 2001. EMS professionals around the country are looking at the New Fairfield move as a possible forerunner of things to come in their locales.

EMT-Basic

Most EMTs hold only basic certification, known as EMT-Basic, or EMT-Ambulance. EMT-Basic training consists of 100 to 120 hours of classroom work plus 10 hours of internship in a hospital emergency room. Training is available in all 50 states and the District of Columbia and is offered by police, fire, and health departments, in hospitals, and as a nondegree course in colleges and universities. The section on certification later in this chapter gives specific guidelines on how to become certified as an EMT-Basic.

EMT-Basics can assess vital signs, including pulse, blood pressure, and respiration; control bleeding; administer CPR; treat shock victims; immobilize and splint fractures; apply bandages; treat and assist heart attack victims; and conduct emergency childbirth. Students learn to use and care for common emergency equipment, such as backboards, suction devices, oxygen delivery systems, and stretchers. The EMT-Basic course also includes training in dispatch language and terminology, to ensure appropriate correspondence with advanced dispatchers.

According to a study in the *Journal of Emergency Medical Services*, the EMT-Basic, or EMT-Ambulance, average salary is $31,670. EMT-Basics earn an average of $36,566 annually working with a fire department, $21,381 annually working with a hospital, and $21,614 annually working with a private ambulance service.

EMT-Intermediate

The second level of certification is EMT-Intermediate. People who obtain this level of certification can perform more advanced intensive care procedures, such as using defibrillators to give lifesaving shocks to a stopped heart. EMT-Intermediate training varies from state to state, but includes 35 to 55 hours of additional instruction in patient assessment as well as the use of esophageal airways, intravenous fluids, and antishock garments. You must have successfully completed the EMT-Basic program in order to move to EMT-Intermediate, and you may provide care only in accordance with the level of your certificate. Refresher courses and continuing education are available for EMTs at all levels to aid in recertification.

According to the *Journal of Emergency Medical Services*, the EMT-Intermediate average annual salary was $30,283 in 2000. EMT-Intermediates earned a low of $22,750 on average working for hospitals and a high of $42,289 working for police departments. Those in fire departments were paid an average of $35,860, while those working for ambulance companies made $24,891.

EMT-Paramedic

A growing number of EMTs have attained the highest level of certification as registered EMT-Paramedics. This level of certification can be gained through an associate's degree or certificate program. Training programs for EMT-Paramedics generally last between 750 and 2,000 hours and allow paramedics to give extensive prehospital care. EMT-Paramedics are authorized to administer drugs intravenously and to operate complicated life-support equipment. They can interpret electrocardiograms (EKGs) and perform endotracheal intubations. EMT-Paramedics have first successfully completed the EMT-Intermediate program.

According to the *Journal of Emergency Medical Services*, EMT-Paramedics' average salary in 2000 was $35,689. They earned an average of $42,161 working with fire departments, $31,130 annually in hospitals, and $30,020 with private ambulance services.

EMT Dispatchers

Police, fire, and ambulance dispatchers are the first people the public speaks to when calling for emergency assistance. Many of them are also trained

EMTs. Dispatchers work in police and fire stations, hospitals, and centralized city communications centers. Usually, 911 calls connect first with a police department dispatcher, who handles the police calls and screens the others before transferring them to the appropriate emergency service.

When handling a call, dispatchers carefully question the caller to determine the type, seriousness, and location of the emergency. They then quickly decide on the kind and number of units needed, locate the closest and most suitable emergency service available, and send the team unit to the scene of the emergency. They keep in touch with the unit until the emergency has been handled, in case further instructions are needed. They may also stay in close contact with other service providers; for example; a police dispatcher would monitor the response of the fire department when there is a major fire or monitor an ambulance until it reaches a hospital. Dispatchers also stay in close contact with bystanders and family and often give them lifesaving instructions while they await an ambulance or other emergency vehicle.

EMT dispatchers earn an average of $28,367. If they work for a fire department, that average increases to $31,482; for ambulance services, it decreases to $21,916. Dispatchers employed in hospitals make an average of $34,358, and in police departments they make $28,734.

Firefighter-EMTs

A national trend in the field of fire protection services is the hiring of more and more firefighters who are also certified EMTs. These firefighters work in communities that may not have separate ambulance service, and they provide the important advantage of being able to attend to victims. Firefighter-EMTs respond to a variety of emergencies in addition to fires. For example, they assist victims of natural disasters and spills of hazardous materials, and they provide emergency medical services to heart attack, stroke, and choking victims. They assess, manage, and administer treatment to ill or injured people on the way to hospitals or other medical facilities, most often in a life-support unit or an ambulance.

See the list below for firefighter salaries in a number of locations to get an idea of what you can expect (figures are from the Labor Relations Information System; for the most recently compiled numbers, check out its website at www.lris.com). If you are considering this career path and you find that your state comes in on the low end of the pay scale, you might want to consider relocating to an area of the country in which firefighters are better paid. You can also find recent salary information in the annual publication entitled *Municipal Year Book*, found in the reference department of your local public library.

Location	Annual Salary
San Jose, California	$57,888
Anchorage, Alaska	$56,304
Jersey City, New Jersey	$55,824
Schaumburg, Illinois	$53,928
Pensacola, Florida	$29,100
Louisville, Kentucky	$27,864
Pontiac, Michigan	$20,940
Monroe, Louisiana	$15,360

Police Officer-EMTs

Police officer-EMTs provide emergency victim support until an ambulance with additional EMTs arrives on the scene. They spend most of their time on patrol, carrying little or no medical equipment. Police officer-EMTs are often the first responders to an incident and can provide emergency services such as CPR. They are also trained to comfort family members and victims, help control crowds and other bystanders, control disorderly patients in dangerous situations, preserve evidence, and lift and move patients. Police officers who train to become EMTs can provide a wider range of services to crime victims and are therefore more marketable as employees and receive higher salaries than officers without the additional certification.

If you are considering becoming a police officer-EMT and are under 21 years of age (the age at which hiring at most police departments begins), you can become an EMT-Basic or EMT-Intermediate in order to gain experience. When you reach the age at which you can apply to police departments, you'll have an edge over the competition.

According to the Bureau of Labor Statistics, the median annual salary for police officers in 1998 was $37,710. Expect to earn more for your additional training as an EMT.

On the Job

The Automated External Defibrillator (AED)

AEDs are portable lifesaving systems used to shock someone back to life after his or her heart has stopped beating. They are used by all levels of certified EMTs, meaning that early defibrillation is available to almost anyone who is met by an emergency response team. Most EMT courses include AED training; however, if it is not included in the standard training course, outside training is available. The use of AEDs is promoted throughout emergency medical facilities.

Air Medical Transport

Air transport EMT-Paramedics work in helicopters and airplanes. They must meet specific requirements, including the completion of three years' experience as a street EMT-Paramedic and proficiency with advanced life support (ALS) interfacility transfers. Most air transport EMTs are also required to have current advanced cardiac life support (ACLS) as well as pediatric advanced life support (PALS) certification. Those interested in this type of work should also consider obtaining prehospital trauma life support training, neonatal resuscitation provider certification, and hazardous materials training. These specialized courses, plus any other medical skills, can greatly improve your chances of getting hired.

Air transport paramedics move patients from the scene of an accident to the nearest hospital or trauma center. Additionally, they work on helicopters and airplanes that routinely fly all types of critical-care patients from one medical facility to another. People who need this service range from those who may be unable to fly on commercial airlines to patients that may need to go across town, across the nation, or somewhere internationally in order to return home or get the medical care they need. Pilots on these flights are also certified EMT-Paramedics.

Armed Forces EMTs

If you're considering enlisting in the Armed Forces—the Army, Navy, Air Force, Marines, or Coast Guard—to become an EMT or get training in pararescue, you should learn as much as you can about military life before making your decision. Speak to those you know who have military experience, talk to a local recruiter (without signing anything at first), and visit these websites:

U.S. Army	www.goarmy.com	1-800-USA-ARMY
U.S. Air Force	www.af.mil	1-800-423-USAF
U.S. Navy	www.navy.mil	1-800-USA-NAVY
U.S. Marines	www.usmc.mil	1-800-MARINES
U.S. Coast Guard	www.uscg.mil	1-800-GET-USCG

The websites are very helpful. You can talk online with recruiters without giving your name, find out about enlistment bonuses, and even read about what to expect during basic training. By visiting each site, you can compare tuition assistance programs, minimum length of service, and other details (for instance, the Coast Guard is the only branch of the military that opens all specialties, including combat ones, to women). There are also more general military sites, such as www.militaryinfo.com and www.defenselink.com, which can be good sources of information.

Military bases need emergency medical services, air rescue, and fire protection just as civilian communities do. However, the military employs enlisted men and women, as well as federal civilian personnel, to protect their people and property, instead of relying on local departments. Since the duties of military EMTs are similar to those of municipal EMTs, a job in the military offers good experience for someone who wants to apply for a municipal job after completing the military enlistment period.

Four Routes to Service

There are four different routes to serving your country in the military:

1. enlisting
2. attending a military academy
3. getting an ROTC scholarship
4. joining the Reserves or National Guard

All these routes can provide the military experience and EMT training that can help your future career, but there are advantages and disadvantages to each. If you enlist, you can spend as little as two years with the military, gain some college credits (often at no cost to you), and come away with money to complete your education as well as work experience employers look for. Military academies are highly competitive, and although you will get a four-year degree at their expense, you will also have a commission, meaning you will serve in the military for a specified period of time after graduation. This is also true of ROTC (Reserve Officers' Training Corps) programs, although you will have a choice of where to attend school. The Reserves or National Guard are the fourth route, offering some money to help pay for schooling while requiring part-time service in the military branch of your choice.

Enlistment Requirements

While there are some variations between branches of the service, there are certain general requirements you will have to meet in order to enlist. You must

- be between 18 and 34 years of age (if 17, you must have a parent's or a guardian's permission)
- be a U.S. citizen (or resident alien in the case of the Coast Guard)
- have a high school diploma or GED (general equivalency diploma) (college credit can sometimes be a substitute)
- be drug-free
- have a clean arrest record

You can request application documents and speak with recruiters online, but eventually you will meet in person with a recruiter. The outcome of this meeting is supposed to be a signed contract between you and the military, so it is of utmost importance that you ask questions and do not sign until you are sure you understand exactly what will be required of you.

Ask about the service and its benefits: salaries, enlistment bonuses, postings, and educational opportunities, including financial aid for college. (See the table below for the basic salaries of various grades of enlisted personnel in all the service branches.) The recruiter will also ask about your education, physical and mental health, goals, interests, hobbies, and life experience. You should mention your desire to receive EMT training and to work as an EMT. You should be able to get a written agreement guaranteeing your placement in the emergency services area.

You will be required to take and pass the Armed Services Vocational Aptitude Battery (ASVAB) test prior to enlisting. After you are accepted into the military, you will need to complete 6 to 11 weeks of basic training and 10 to 20 weeks of additional technical school training to prepare for your career in the military. You may choose from a variety of educational programs, such as emergency medical care or pararescue training.

Enlistment by Branch

Branch of Service	Terms of Enlistment
Army	2, 4, or 6 years
Navy	3, 4, 5, or 6 years
Air Force	4 or 6 years
Marine Corps	3, 4, or 5 years

The Pay Scale

Salaries for military EMTs, air transport EMTs, firefighter-EMTs, and pararescuers are on the same scale as for other military jobs. The salary you'll receive depends on the years of experience and the grade level or rank you have obtained. See the table below for a range of monthly salaries in the military as of January 1, 2000. The dollar amounts in the table combine basic pay, the basic allowance for quarters, the basic allowance for subsistence, and the average variable housing allowance. They also include the tax advantage from untaxed allowances. The figures do not include the average overseas housing allowance or the overseas cost-of-living allowance.

The 2000 Military Pay Chart

Grade							Years of Service							
	<2	2	3	4	6	8	10	12	14	16	18	20	22	24
Commissioned Officers														
O-10	8214.90	8503.80	8503.80	8503.80	8503.80	8830.20	8830.20	9319.50	9319.50	9986.40	9986.40	10655.10	10655.10	10655.10
O-9	7280.70	7471.50	7630.50	7630.50	7630.50	7824.60	7824.60	8150.10	8150.10	8830.20	8830.20	9319.50	9319.50	9319.50
O-8	6594.30	6792.30	6953.10	6953.10	6953.10	7471.50	7471.50	7824.60	7824.60	8150.10	8503.80	8830.20	9048.00	9048.00
O-7	5479.50	5851.80	5851.80	5851.80	6114.60	6114.60	6468.90	6468.90	6792.30	7471.50	7985.40	7985.40	7985.40	7985.40
O-6	4061.10	4461.60	4754.40	4754.40	4754.40	4754.40	4754.40	4754.40	4916.10	5693.10	5983.80	6114.60	6468.90	6687.30
O-5	3248.40	3813.90	4077.90	4077.90	4077.90	4077.90	4200.30	4427.10	4723.80	5077.50	5368.30	5531.10	5724.60	5724.60
O-4	2737.80	3333.90	3556.20	3556.20	3622.20	3781.80	4040.40	4267.50	4461.60	4658.10	4785.90	4785.90	4785.90	4785.90
O-3	2544.00	2844.30	3041.10	3364.80	3525.90	3652.20	3850.20	4040.40	4139.10	4139.10	4139.10	4139.10	4139.10	4139.10
O-2	2218.80	2423.10	2910.90	3009.00	3071.10	3071.10	3071.10	3071.10	3071.10	3071.10	3071.10	3071.10	3071.10	3071.10
O-1	1926.30	2004.90	2423.10	2423.10	2423.10	2423.10	2423.10	2423.10	2423.10	2423.10	2423.10	2423.10	2423.10	2423.10
Commissioned Officers with over 4 years active duty service as an enlisted member or warrant officer														
O-3E	0.00	0.00	0.00	0.00	3525.90	3652.20	3850.20	4040.40	4200.30	4200.30	4200.30	4200.30	4200.30	4200.30
O-2E	0.00	0.00	0.00	0.00	3071.10	3168.60	3333.90	3461.40	3556.20	3556.20	3556.20	3556.20	3556.20	3556.20
O-1E	0.00	0.00	0.00	2423.10	2588.40	2683.80	2781.30	2877.60	3009.00	3009.00	3009.00	3009.00	3009.00	3009.00
Warrant Officers														
W-5	0.00	0.00	0.00	0.00	0.00	0.00	0.00	0.00	0.00	0.00	0.00	4423.80	4591.20	4724.10
W-4	2592.00	2781.30	2781.30	2844.30	2974.20	3105.00	3235.50	3461.40	3622.20	3749.40	3850.20	3874.10	4107.00	4235.10
W-3	2355.90	2555.40	2555.40	2588.40	2618.70	2810.40	2974.20	3071.10	3168.60	3263.40	3364.80	3495.90	3622.20	3622.20
W-2	2063.40	2232.60	2232.60	2297.40	2423.10	2555.40	2652.60	2749.80	2844.30	2944.50	3041.10	3136.80	3263.40	3263.40
W-1	1719.00	1971.00	1971.00	2135.90	2232.60	2328.00	2423.10	2522.70	2618.70	2716.20	2810.40	2910.90	2910.90	2910.90

The 2000 Military Pay Chart (Continued)

Enlisted Members

Grade	\<2	2	3	4	6	8	10	12	14	16	18	20	22	24
								Years of Service						
E-9	0.00	0.00	0.00	0.00	0.00	0.00	3015.30	3083.40	3152.70	3225.60	3298.20	3361.50	3537.90	3675.60
E-8	0.00	0.00	0.00	0.00	0.00	2528.40	2601.60	2669.70	2739.00	2811.60	2875.50	2946.30	3119.40	3258.00
E-7	1765.80	1906.20	1976.10	2045.70	2115.60	2182.80	2252.70	2323.20	2427.90	2496.90	2566.20	2599.50	2774.40	2912.40
E-6	1518.90	1655.70	1724.40	1797.50	1865.40	1932.60	2003.40	2106.60	2172.90	2242.80	2277.00	2277.00	2277.00	2277.00
E-5	1332.60	1450.50	1521.00	1587.30	1691.70	1761.00	1830.00	1898.10	1932.60	1932.60	1932.60	1932.60	1932.60	1932.60
E-4	1242.90	1312.80	1390.20	1497.30	1556.70	1556.70	1556.70	1556.70	1556.70	1556.70	1556.70	1556.70	1556.70	1556.70
E-3	1171.50	1235.70	1284.60	1335.90	1335.90	1335.90	1335.90	1335.90	1335.90	1335.90	1335.90	1335.90	1335.90	1335.90
E-2	1127.40	1127.40	1127.40	1127.40	1127.40	1127.40	1127.40	1127.40	1127.40	1127.40	1127.40	1127.40	1127.40	1127.40
E-1>4	1005.60	1005.60	1005.60	1005.60	1005.60	1005.60	1005.60	1005.60	1005.60	1005.60	1005.60	1005.60	1005.60	1005.60
E-1<4	930.30	0.00	0.00	0.00	0.00	0.00	0.00	0.00	0.00	0.00	0.00	0.00	0.00	0.00

Key to Military Ranks

Army Ranks:
E-1: Recruit
E-2: Private
E-3: Private First Class
E-4: Corporal/Specialist
E-5: Sergeant
E-6: Staff Sergeant
E-7: Sergeant First Class
E-8: Master Sergeant
E-9: Sergeant Major

Navy Ranks:
E-1: Airman or Seaman or Fireman or Construction Recruit
E-2: Airman or Seaman or Fireman or Construction Apprentice
E-3: Airman or Seaman or Fireman or Construction
E-4: Petty Officer 3rd Class
E-5: Petty Officer 2nd Class
E-6: Petty Officer 1st Class
E-7: Chief Petty Officer
E-8: Senior Chief Petty Officer
E-9: Master Chief Petty Officer

Air Force Ranks:
E-1: Airman basic
E-2: Airman
E-3: Airman 1st Class
E-4: Senior Airman
E-5: Staff Sergeant
E-6: Technical Sergeant
E-7: Master Sergeant
E-8: Senior Master Sergeant
E-9: Chief Master Sergeant

Marine Ranks:
E-1: Private
E-2: Private First Class
E-3: Lance Corporal
E-4: Corporal
E-5: Sergeant
E-6: Staff Sergeant
E-7: Gunnery Sergeant
E-8: Either Master Sergeant or 1st Sergeant
E-9: Master Gunnery Sergeant or Sergeant Major

Coast Guard Ranks:
E-1: Recruit
E-2: Fireman or Seaman Apprentice
E-3: Fireman or Seaman
E-4: Petty Officer 3rd Class
E-5: Petty Officer 2nd Class
E-6: Petty Officer 1st Class
E-7: Chief Petty Officer
E-8: Senior Chief Petty Officer

STEPS TO BECOMING AN EMT

If you are considering a career as an EMT, begin preparing for future success now. The following list details the steps necessary for the achievement of your goal:

Graduate from high school or obtain a GED

The first step to becoming an EMT is to graduate from high school or secure its equivalency; a GED can be obtained from most adult education centers in your area.

Consider volunteering

There are a number of volunteer opportunities that can help you in two ways: (1) you will gain a hands-on view of the emergency medical services field, which may aid in your future career decisions, and (2) you will have positive experience to add to your resume. Ask local ambulance companies and hospitals about their volunteer programs, and check into organizations such as the American Red Cross.

Complete a training program

Consult Chapter 2 and the suggested resources for information about how to evaluate training programs. Locate the programs that suit your needs and choose one or more to complete.

Conduct a job search

Read Chapter 4 carefully, and follow the advice it contains. There are many different ways to search for work as an EMT and many different types of positions. Arm yourself with as much information as possible to help you land the job you want.

EMT-B Peter Herslow suggests:

> The advice I would give to anyone starting out would be to ride on the ambulance before you get all of your schooling, because then you will know if you like it and can do it. Not everyone can do the emergency stuff. For those who like it, it can really get in your blood!

EMT CERTIFICATION

Once you have completed a training program, the time it takes to meet state certification requirements can be one to two years. It is important to meet these requirements in a timely manner; allowing too much time to pass could mean you'd need to repeat the training. EMT-Intermediate David Saucer from Chicago, Illinois, describes obtaining certification as "the most stressful part of the job. I was so nervous during the test, I couldn't believe it. I wasn't half as nervous during my job interview."

Once all the requirements of your EMT program have been met, you will need to contact the National Registry of Emergency Medical Technicians (NREMT) or your local state registry to obtain an application and find out where you can take the certification test. Alternately, you may find that you need to make individual arrangements to take the exam in your state. The registration fee for the NREMT application is $15 for the Basic and $35 for the Intermediate or the Paramedic. There is a different certification exam for each EMT level.

There are several different texts available, some of them based on the NREMT test, to help you study for the written certification examination. (A list of test preparation materials can be found in Appendix C.) Whether you will be taking a state test or the NREMT test, you will be learning and studying similar material.

There are minimum requirements that must be met before you can apply for certification. You must:

- ▶ be 18 years of age or older
- ▶ have successfully completed (within the last two years) a state-approved EMT-Basic (or previous level) training program
- ▶ truthfully complete the felony statement
- ▶ submit current CPR credentials
- ▶ submit a completed application
- ▶ pay the registration fee ($15 for Basic, $35 for Intermediate or Paramedic)

EMT-Basic Exam

The National Registry's EMT-Basic exam consists of two parts, the written and the practical exams. The written exam is composed of 150 multiple-choice questions. Exam content is based on tasks identified in the

EMT-Basic practical analysis conducted by the NREMT. This analysis is the basis of the 1994 national standard EMT-Basic curriculum, which is studied in basic EMT courses. Copies of the practical analysis and a practice exam to aid in preparation are available from the National Registry. Contact it through its website (www.nremt.org) for more information.

The written exam consists of six content areas:

1. patient assessment
2. airway and breathing
3. circulation
4. musculoskeletal, behavioral, neurological, and environmental
5. children and OB-GYN
6. EMS systems: ethical, legal, communications, documentation, safety, triage, and transportation

In order to pass, you must answer at least 105 items correctly, for a minimum score of 70%. Candidates who fail may reapply by submitting a new application with fee and retake the exam. Those who fail three times must successfully complete a 24-hour refresher course before reapplying.

The practical examination consists of several applications of emergency medical procedures. Section I requires verification of your CPR credentials from either the American Heart Association or the American Red Cross. Section II requires your EMT instructor to verify that you have shown a minimal level of competence in 13 key skill areas:

1. patient assessment/management—trauma
2. patient assessment/management—medical
3. cardiac arrest management/AED
4. spinal immobilization—seated patient
5. spinal immobilization—supine patient
6. bag-valve-mask apneic patient with a pulse
7. long bone fracture immobilization
8. joint dislocation immobilization
9. traction splinting
10. bleeding control/shock management
11. upper airway adjuncts and suction

12. mouth-to-mouth with supplemental oxygen

13. supplemental oxygen administration

Section III requires you to submit proof that you have successfully completed a state-approved practical examination. At a minimum, the exam must evaluate your performance in these skills:

Station 1—patient assessment/ management—trauma

Station 2—patient assessment/ management—medical

Station 3—cardiac arrest management/AED

Station 4—spinal immobilization—seated or supine patient

Station 5—bag-valve-mask apneic patient with a pulse

Station 6—random skill station (one of the following): long bone fracture or joint dislocation immobilization, traction splinting, bleeding control/shock management, upper airway adjuncts and suction, mouth-to-mouth with supplemental oxygen, or supplemental oxygen administration

EMT-Intermediate Exam

The National Registry's Intermediate exam also consists of written and practical tests. The written exam is made up of two parts. Part I is the EMT-Basic reassessment of basic skills and knowledge, consisting of 70 multiple-choice questions covering the material presented in the national standard EMT-Basic training curriculum. Part II contains questions derived from the national standard EMT-Intermediate objectives. The 80 multiple-choice questions cover roles and responsibilities, EMS systems, medical legal considerations, medical terminology, EMS communications, general patient assessment and initial management, airway management and ventilation, and assessment and management of shock. As with the Basic exam, you may take the written part of the test up to three times after reapplying and paying the required fee for each retest.

The practical section of the exam consists of five stations designed to simulate emergency situations dealt with by EMTs. The process gives the candidate a chance to display his or her actual abilities and knowledge in five areas:

1. patient assessment/management: perform a head-to-toe assessment of a victim and identify appropriate treatment
2. ventilation management: treat a patient who is not breathing but has a pulse, using simple airway maneuvers, a bag-valve-mask device, supplemental oxygen, and one of the following: EOA, EGTA, combitube, PTL, or endotracheal tube
3. intravenous (IV) therapy: establish an IV in a mannequin's arm
4. spinal immobilization of a seated patient: use appropriate device with proper application
5. random basic skills (two of the following): bleeding/wounds/shock, long bone splinting, traction splinting, and spinal immobilization of a supine patient

The practical exam is graded as pass or fail. Candidates must pass all five stations. If one or two are failed, the candidate may try those stations again on the same day. However, if he or she fails one or both again, all five stations must be completed successfully on another date.

EMT-Paramedic Exam

The EMT-Paramedic written exam asks 180 multiple-choice questions in six areas: patient assessment; airway and breathing; circulation; musculoskeletal, behavioral, neurological and environmental; children and OB-GYN; and EMS systems (ethical, legal, communications, documentation, safety, triage, and transportation).

The practical examination includes six stations designed to test the abilities of the EMT-Paramedic in an out-of-hospital setting. Grading is done on a pass/fail basis; all stations must be passed. If a candidate fails three or fewer stations, he or she may retest them on the same day. Subsequent failure results in a reexamination on all stations on another date after submission of a new application and application fee. The test stations of the practical exam are

1. patient assessment/management
2. ventilatory management
3. cardiac arrest skills
4. IV and medication skills
5. spinal immobilization of a seated patient
6. random basic skills (two of the following): bleeding/wounds/shock, long bone splinting, traction splinting, and spinal immobilization of a supine patient

If a candidate passes one section of the test (written or practical) and fails the other, the passed portion remains valid for one year from the date of the exam. If the failed portion is not completed within that year, the entire exam must be retaken. As with the Basic and Intermediate tests, failure after three full attempts means that the candidate must repeat the appropriate training program before taking another exam.

STATE VERSUS NREMT EXAMS

In some states, the NREMT certification process is the only licensure process for EMTs. Other states have their own testing procedures. Some states offer new EMTs the choice of the National Registry examination or the state's own certification examination, and some may require both. A majority of states accept national registration in place of their own examination for EMTs who relocate there. Both the NREMT and the state tests are based on the same curriculum, which is issued by the U.S. Department of Transportation (DOT), to ensure national standards for training, testing, and continuing education. Certification enables an employer to be sure that EMT candidates have the knowledge and skills to do their job saving lives and preserving health.

SUITABILITY TEST

Conducting a self-evaluation will help you discover whether you possess the qualities most associated with successful EMTs. From the information you've read throughout this chapter, you have learned that EMTs must be physically fit, able to work well under extreme conditions and handle high stress levels, and be compassionate and caring. One EMT describes some likes and dislikes about the job:

> I like being there when someone is needed. I don't really enjoy going on a call to a bad accident, especially since I have a teenager and know many kids around here. But I know I can help get someone to a hospital and I love seeing him or her walk out of the hospital when their car looked like an accordion. I also don't get a lot of sleep when on duty. I'm usually too keyed up to sleep well, and I don't want to sleep through a call. This makes me tired the next day—especially when I have to go to my first job and work all day. Volunteers have regular jobs they have to go to no matter how many calls they ran with the EMS the night before or how few hours of sleep they had.

Begin your evaluation with an honest look at how much training you wish to pursue and commit yourself to; for example, an EMT-Basic certificate usually requires six months to one year of school, depending on the type of program and whether any extra courses, such as ambulance training, are taken. EMT-Paramedic training can take up to two years. Consult Chapter 2 for an in-depth look at the training process.

Next, take an inventory of your skills and areas of interest. What do you do well? What are the skills you most enjoy using? Identify your skills, gifts, and talents, and list them in order of importance.

Now, create a list of all the jobs you've ever had, including summer jobs, volunteer work, part-time jobs, and any freelance or short-term assignments you've done. Do the same for your education, listing the school(s) you attended, your major courses of study, grades, special awards or honors, courses you particularly enjoyed, and extracurricular activities in which you were involved.

Armed with your self-evaluation, honestly consider the following:

► Do you have the desire to help people in immediate need?
► Are you patient and caring with people?
► Are you skilled under extreme pressure?
► Can you put others before yourself?
► Can you work as part of a team?
► Would you like good benefits and a challenging work atmosphere?
► Do you want a variety of tasks and work situations?
► Would you like the chance to save someone's life?
► Are you physically fit, able to lift heavy things?
► Are you mentally fit, able to remain under stress for long periods of time?
► Would you be able to handle death and other terrible situations?

If you are able to answer yes to most of the questions, you have many of the characteristics and skills of a successful EMT. As a final step before committing yourself to working in the emergency medical services field, you may wish to consult with an experienced career counselor. A counselor can give you a series of vocational interest and aptitude tests and interpret and explain the results. Vocational testing and counseling can be found in the guidance departments of high schools, vocational schools, and colleges. Some local offices of state employment services affiliated with the federal employment service offer free counseling. Counselors will not tell you what to do, but they can help guide you in your search for a specialization.

INSIDE TRACK

Barry McClung
Paramedic and Crew Chief
North Blanco County EMS and Blanco EMS
Johnson City, Texas

I started out with a small volunteer fire department and a combination paid/volunteer rescue squad in Pennsylvania, but the majority of my career has been spent in the Houston and San Antonio regions. September 2000 marks my 20th year in EMS, and during that time I have worked for public agencies as well as private companies while working my way up from an EMT-Basic to the level of Paramedic. Now I work with North Blanco County EMS, which is a volunteer department, as well as with Blanco EMS, a paid/volunteer department.

I love my career. I haven't ever regretted the choices I've made. I like the ability to make a difference, to be able to stabilize someone long enough to get them to definitive care. Using the tools and technologies of a modern-day paramedic, I can prevent further damage in cases such as a cardiac arrest or during an active myocardial infection. I often feel good about the chance I have to provide comfort to the family of the victim, even if I cannot do much for the patient. One of the hardest parts of the job is dealing with injured children, especially in the case of senseless injuries like those caused by child abuse or neglect.

North Blanco EMS runs 12-hour shifts and Blanco runs the standard 24–48 schedule. Too much of this time is spent doing paperwork rather than running calls, and I do more paperwork nowadays than ever before. In order to keep up with current developments and innovations, I subscribe to several professional journals, read textbooks, study equipment operating manuals, attend conferences and classes, and take on-line continuing education courses. I do all this in order to be able to perform to the best of my ability, as well as to protect myself from lawsuits. Another major responsibility is cleaning and maintenance—I spend a lot of time caring for the station, the truck, and all the equipment.

The innovations in the field have enabled EMTs to handle a wider variety of conditions and provide better care. The quality of the training has improved: it has become more accurate, accessible, and pertinent. We have better protocols, better equipment, and better ambulances. The use of air ambulances is more widespread; cellular phones have made EMS-to-hospital communications more secure and reliable; and some services even have live-action video feed connections with their primary medical facilities.

I would advise anyone who wants to build a career in EMS to go to college and get an EMS degree as soon as possible, because academic qualifications are the way of the future. Personally, I waited much too long, and now I have to play catch-up. Never turn down any opportunity to acquire new knowledge or improve what you already have.

CHAPTER two

BECOMING A CANDIDATE: EDUCATION

THIS CHAPTER discusses training programs: how to evaluate them and how to choose the right one for you. You'll find out about entrance requirements, and you'll be given some key questions to ask about the training program you're interested in. You will also find sample course descriptions, and Appendix D contains an extensive directory of schools that offer EMT-Basic, EMT-Intermediate, and EMT-Paramedic courses.

ALL JOBS in the EMS field require some period of training in order for you to gain knowledge of the necessary lifesaving procedures. Your training will take place in the classroom, where you will learn proper terminology and techniques, as well as in a clinical setting involving direct patient treatment and operating equipment. In order to enter the EMT field, you must successfully complete your training program and then take exams to obtain the appropriate level certificate. Only after you are certified can you actually begin work in your chosen career.

MAKING DECISIONS ABOUT TRAINING

You have read descriptions of many of the jobs available to EMTs, based on the level of EMT certification. Perhaps you already know which type of position you want. That makes deciding on a training program easier: find the program that will best prepare you for the exact type of job you'll be applying for. You may be interested in neonatal emergency care or wilderness EMS work; there are training courses specifically geared toward these specialties. If you're planning on a job that combines law enforcement or firefighting with EMT skills, you will look at programs that can give you all the training you'll need.

If you're not yet sure which type of EMT position interests you, look at the programs that prepare students to pass the EMT-Basic exam. No matter what kind of work you end up doing in the emergency services field, you will at the very least need basic training and an EMT-Basic certificate. Once you're working, you will need to get continuing education credits to keep your certificate. At that time, you can opt to go for the next level of certification or specialize. You'll have had time in the field to check out the possibilities.

If you'd rather try to focus your education search more narrowly from the start, use the personal evaluation you created at the end of Chapter 1 to consider the following questions. Though you may not know the answers right away, the questions can help you tailor your career goals to a specific EMT position and then choose the appropriate training program.

► Do I need a job now or can I wait and gain greater experience through education?
► How much time am I willing to devote to my education before getting a job as an EMT?
► What schools are in my area?
► Can I or do I want to relocate in order to attend the school that best meets my needs?
► Do I want to specialize in one area of EMT work?
► What kind of certification or degree do I want to complete?
► In what kind of facility do I want to work?

▶ What is the salary level I'd like to have?

▶ What kinds of coworkers would I like to have?

These questions may be the most important to ask yourself. They will determine what kind of job you will actually train for. You should research career options by visiting hospital ambulance services, fire stations, police departments, private ambulance services, and other health organizations in your area to actually see the work environment and the staff. Also research the salary options for the job you want from the health centers in your area, because the salary descriptions in Chapter 1 are based on national averages rather than specific regional information.

While it's important to set goals for your career, be open to trying or researching work environments that you might not have originally considered. There's also no need to lock yourself into something permanently after school. Once you are certified as an EMT-Basic, you can begin work and then possibly decide to further your education in order to move up in status and salary.

HIGH SCHOOL PREPARATION

If you haven't yet completed high school, you can take courses that will help you to prepare for becoming an EMT while you are still in school. First, concentrate on basic skills such as reading comprehension, writing, computer literacy, and basic mathematics and science. If you are planning to enter college for an EMT-Paramedic course of study, you'll want to follow a college prep model. This includes four years of English (composition and literature), three years of math, and at least two years of science, a foreign language, and history. If you're planning to enroll in an EMT-Basic certificate program, take as many of the following classes as possible:

▶ health

▶ science

▶ driver education or defensive driving

▶ English

▶ physical education (PE)

▶ computer training

▶ Spanish or another language

By building a strong educational foundation while still in high school, you'll increase your chances of succeeding in the next phase of your training, whether it's for a certificate, an associate's degree, or an on-the-job training program.

IN THE NEWS

High School EMT Training

Rockwall High School in Rockwall, Texas, offers its students an innovative EMT class. Students are exposed to the medical field, and if they get a score of at least 80 in the class they are eligible to take the state's EMT exam. Once the students finish their semester in the classroom, they receive supervised, hands-on experience with a local ambulance service and a hospital emergency room.

EMT TRAINING PROGRAM ENTRANCE REQUIREMENTS

To be admitted into a basic EMT training program, applicants must be at least 18 years old, have a high school diploma or GED, and have a valid driver's license. Other requirements for the various levels of the EMT courses vary slightly from state to state. Many incoming students need to complete entrance exams, such as the Science Placement Test (SPT) or the College Placement Test (CPT), which help to determine placement in courses. These tests evaluate reading, writing, and math skills. Other tests used in admitting applicants to programs may include the College Board SATs (Scholastic Achievement Tests), which you may have taken already in high school (test scores are valid for a limited number of years, so you may need to retake them) or the American College Test (ACT).

Most schools will ask that you have your high school send a transcript detailing your courses and grades during the application process. Your grade point average (GPA) may be used to determine whether or not you will be accepted into the program. GEDs are an acceptable substitute for a high school degree at most schools. You may also be asked to supply recommendation letters and personal statements.

Another entrance requirement is the right attitude. Jeanine L. Hoffman, an EMT-Basic instructor from Landisville, Pennsylvania, says:

> Students *must* have a willingness to learn, the ability to arrive on time at every class, and the ability to change their way of thinking. Many people think of EMS as how they see it on *COPS* or *Rescue 911*. Once they get into class, they need to change those misconceptions and see the realities of EMT work, such as the facts that we can't save everyone and that some people try to hurt us when we try to help them. I like to see every student enter class with the desire to help others, a respect for other people, and a mature attitude toward their studies. Things like a background in medicine or fire service are nice but not needed. We can teach the skills, but the attitude is something the students need to have already.

Some schools also require students to take a physical and have blood work done to check for any contagious diseases. You will also have to provide proof that your immunizations are up to date. Students may have to purchase health insurance if they are not already covered. The school should offer a liability or malpractice insurance policy at a small fee to its students.

TYPES OF TRAINING PROGRAMS

The educational requirements for EMT occupations range from 100 or more hours for an EMT-Basic training course to 750 or more hours for an EMT-Paramedic certificate program or an associate's degree. Requirements vary from state to state, with some requiring over 50 credits for basic training and others less than 15. Training for entry-level positions at the basic and intermediate levels is offered in community colleges, technical schools, colleges, universities, the Armed Forces, and some police and fire academies. Programs provide both classroom and clinical instruction. For paramedic and specialty training, courses are most often found in colleges and universities. Below are described the three levels of EMT certification, with the training requirements of each. Sample course lists and costs of education are included.

EMT-Basic Training Program

EMT-Basic training involves 100 to 180 hours of classroom work and internship in clinical and field settings. These programs are offered at hundreds of sites throughout the country, with plenty of variation. For instance, the University of Iowa offers the training as a full-time, 40-hour-per-week course that can be completed in just four weeks. The program costs $500, and tuition assistance is available. Most other programs involve just a few hours per week and take about nine months to complete. If you are holding down a full-time job while getting your education, the pace of the program will be of great interest to you.

Check the directory at the end of this book for a listing of schools across the United States offering EMT courses. Then search the Internet with a search engine such as Google.com, using the term *emergency medical technician*, to find specifics on hundreds of other training programs around the country.

Here is an example of a two-semester EMT-Basic course from a community college in Oregon. Instruction consists of four hours of lecture and three hours of lab work per week for 12 weeks. Students must also participate in an ambulance ride-along and rotations in an emergency department. The course costs residents of Oregon or any state bordering it $351, plus $100 in lab fees. Other nonresidents pay $1,305 plus $100 in lab fees. Students who complete the course successfully are then eligible to take the EMT-Basic licensing exam.

First Semester

Introduction to Emergency Medical Care

Covers medical, legal, and ethical issues; anatomy and physiology; lifting and moving patients; well-being of the EMT-Basic; and baseline vital signs

Airway

Covers signs of adequate and inadequate breathing, structures of the respiratory system, suctioning, artificial ventilation, and the bag-valve-mask system

Scene Size-Up

Covers patient assessment, initial assessment, focused history and physical exam, ongoing assessment, communications, documentation, and behavioral emergencies

Second Semester

General Pharmacology

Covers respiratory emergencies, cardiovascular emergencies, diabetes/altered mental states, allergies, poisoning/overdose, environmental emergencies, and obstetrics/gynecology

Bleeding and Shock

Covers soft-tissue injuries, musculoskeletal care, and injuries to head and spine

Infants and Children

Covers anatomy and physiology, respiratory distress versus respiratory failure, foreign body airway obstruction, shock, seizures, and indicators of possible child abuse and neglect

Ambulance Operations

Covers medical and nonmedical equipment needed for calls; phases of ambulance calls; state laws pertaining to operation of an ambulance; factors contributing to unsafe driving conditions; preparing an ambulance for the next response; and the distinction between cleaning, disinfecting, and sterilization

Gaining Access

Covers the purpose of extraction, protecting a patient during extraction, simple and complex access, and the role of an EMT-Basic during extraction

EMT-Intermediate Training Program

An EMT-Intermediate student must have successfully completed an EMT-Basic course, have current CPR certification, and have proof of up-to-date immunizations for such diseases as measles and rubella. The EMT-Intermediate course at a technical college in Wisconsin includes 60 hours of classroom instruction, a minimum of 40 hours of supervised clinical experience in a hospital, and a minimum of 20 hours of supervised field experience on an ambulance. The college charges $184.50 for residents of Wisconsin and $1,444.05 for nonresidents.

The EMT-Intermediate course is offered for three credits and is taught in a series of 20 lessons, as follows:

Lesson 1: Roles and responsibilities (EMS systems, medico-legal issues, infection control, communicable diseases)

Lesson 2: EMS communication (rescue and MCIs, stress and CISD, medical terminology)

Lesson 3: Anatomy and physiology

Lesson 4: Advanced patient assessment

Lesson 5: Practical skills lab

Lesson 6: Airway management

Lesson 7: Practical skills lab

Lesson 8: Pathophysiology of shock, shock/trauma resuscitation

Lesson 9: Practical skills lab

Lesson 10: Pharmacology

Lesson 11: Practical skills lab

Lesson 12: Trauma (kinetics, head, neck, spine, body cavity, musculoskeletal, soft tissue injuries)

Lesson 13: Cardiac emergencies

Lesson 14: Endocrine and metabolic nervous systems, anaphylaxis

Lesson 15: Gastrointestinal, genitourinary, reproductive

Lesson 16: Toxicology/substance abuse, (behavioral/psychological, environmental)

Lesson 17: Pediatric, gynecological, obstetrics, neonatal

Lesson 18: Geriatrics (practical skills practice)

Lesson 19: Final written exam

Lesson 20: Final practical testing

EMT-Paramedic Training Program

Training programs for EMT-Paramedics generally take between 750 and 2,000 hours of study, and you can enroll in a certificate or associate's degree program. Here is an example of a two-year program for EMT-Paramedics from a college in Nebraska. It consists of 50 credit hours, which may be taken for college credit, and costs either $6,000 for a certificate or $303 per credit hour for college credit. Prerequisites for the EMT-Paramedic course include successful completion of an EMT-Intermediate program, current CPR certification, and proof of up-to-date immunizations.

Course Number	Course Name	Credit Hours
EMS 200	ANATOMY AND PHYSIOLOGY—PRINCIPLES AND PRACTICE	5

This course is a comprehensive study of the human body focusing on anatomical structure and physiological processes. The anatomy and physiology studies are based on the requirements of the DOT (Department of Transportation) national standard curriculum for paramedic practice. Laboratory experience will include 15 hours of cadaver study.

EMS 201	INTRODUCTION TO PARAMEDICINE	2

An introduction to paramedic practice. Students will be introduced to professional roles and responsibilities, medical/legal and ethical considerations, and the overall well-being of the paramedic as a prehospital provider in emergency medical care.

EMS 202	AIRWAY MANAGEMENT AND VENTILATION	2

This course will focus on the anatomy and physiology of the respiratory system, its components, and emergency medical management, including assisting ventilation, endotracheal intubation, and needle cricothyrotomy. Enrichment of this section will also include clinical/field experience.

EMS 203	PATIENT ASSESSMENT—TECHNIQUES OF PHYSICAL EXAM	3

Patient Assessment—Techniques of Physical Exam is designed to expand the student's knowledge and skill mastery of assessment as it pertains to care of the emergent and the nonemergent patient. This course will focus on a complete assessment and emergency treatment of the sick and injured. Enrichment of this section will also include clinical/field experience.

EMS 204	CLINICAL PRACTICUM I	1

Clinical Practicum I includes 15 hours of human cadaver experience with the anatomy and physiology instructor, 18 hours with anesthesia professionals performing live intubations, 12 hours with respiratory therapy professionals administering treatments, and 5 hours with professionals from the phlebotomy lab and/or IV team for blood draws and establishing intravenous lines.

EMS 205	INTRODUCTION TO PATHOPHYSIOLOGY AND PHARMACOLOGY	4

Pathophysiology begins with a major focus on cellular function and pathology, including inflammation, infection, immune response, metabolism, and fluid disequilibrium. These concepts serve as a foundation for the course as alterations in various bodily functions are examined. Alterations in body fluid and electrolytic homeostasis, fluid acid/base balance, and gastrointestinal, urinary, respiratory, cardiac, endocrine, and neurological functions are emphasized. The paramedic student will also be introduced to pharmacological principles. The various drug classifications and the general characteristics of drugs within a class are examined, focusing on the complete analysis of pharmacokinetics and pharmacodynamics, including theories of drug action, the drug-response relationship, and factors altering drug responses and drug interactions.

Course Number	Course Name	Credit Hours
EMS 206	MEDICAL PRACTICE I—CARDIOLOGY	5

This course is based on the DOT curriculum for paramedics and the American Heart Association's ACLS course. Emphasis is placed on recognition and management of cardiac emergencies, including chest pain management, rhythm analysis, defibrillation, synchronized cardioversion, and transcutaneous pacing. Enrichment of this section will also include clinical/field experience.

EMS 207	MEDICAL PRACTICE II	5

Medical Practice II will be taught in conjunction with the national standard curriculum for paramedics and the National Association of EMTs advanced medical life support course. This course is designed for recognition and emergency treatment of the medically ill patient. Students will learn specific pathophysiology for medical disease processes and for the acutely ill patient. Enrichment of this section will also include clinical/field experience.

EMS 208	CLINICAL PRACTICUM II	2

Clinical Practicum II will provide students with clinical experience in the areas of critical care (32 hours), labor and delivery (16 hours), psychiatric services (8 hours) and emergency room (50 hours). Students will be assigned to specific professionals who have expertise in these areas. Students will demonstrate various skills outlined in the field/clinical policies.

EMS 209	FIELD EXPERIENCE I	1

Field Experience I is designed to introduce students to scene management, patient assessment and treatment, documentation, communication, and interaction with family and ancillary health care personnel as these skills pertain to prehospital emergency care. Emphasis is on interfacing with patients, hospitals, families, the general public, and other public service personnel. Students will have a minimum of 50 hours in the field, working with various fire department/ambulance services under the direct supervision of an approved field preceptor. Students will demonstrate various skills outlined in the field/clinical policies.

EMS 210	SPECIAL CONSIDERATIONS OF PARAMEDIC PRACTICE	3

This course examines special considerations of the young and old. Emphasis is placed on patients with special needs and challenges and on interventions for the critically ill patient. Focuses are on neonatology, pediatrics, geriatrics, and acute interventions for the chronically ill patient.

EMS 211	TRAUMA PRACTICE AND ASSESSMENT BASED MANAGEMENT	3

Trauma practice and assessment-based management will focus on the recognition and treatment of trauma patients, including management and use of the trauma system. By the completion of this class, students will be proficient in patient assessment and management of the critical and noncritical trauma patient. Students will master skills of rapid extrication, spinal immobilization, splinting of extremities, chest needle decompression, and trauma intubation, including rapid sequence intubation.

Course Number	Course Name	Credit Hours
EMS 212	SPECIAL OPERATIONS FOR PARAMEDICS	1

Special Operations emphasizes medical incident command and rescue operations. This course will also introduce students to hazardous material incidences and crime scene awareness.

EMS 213	CLINICAL PRACTICUM III	2

Clinical Practicum III will provide students with clinical experience in the areas of pediatrics (24 hours), triage (20 hours), and emergency room (56 hours). Students will be assigned to specific professionals who have expertise in these areas. Students will demonstrate various skills outlined in the field/clinical policies.

EMS 214	FIELD EXPERIENCE II	1

Field Experience II is designed to introduce students to scene management, patient assessment and treatment, documentation, communication, and interaction with family and ancillary health care personnel as these skills pertain to prehospital emergency care. Emphasis is on interfacing with patients, hospitals, families, the general public, and other public service personnel. Students will have a minimum of 50 hours in the field, working with various fire department/ambulance services under the direct supervision of an approved field preceptor. Students will demonstrate various skills outlined in the field/clinical policies.

EMS 215	PROFESSIONAL CERTIFICATIONS	4

Completion of the four two-day courses will give the paramedic student special certifications in advanced cardiac life support, prehospital trauma life support, pediatric advanced life support, and advanced medical life support. These certifications will be valuable for professional practice in the field and advancement in a paramedic career.

EMS 216	CLINICAL PRACTICUM IV	1

Clinical Practicum IV will provide students with clinical experience in the area of emergency room (50 hours). Students will be assigned to specific professionals who have expertise in these areas. Students will demonstrate various skills outlined in the field/clinical policies.

EMS 217	FIELD EXPERIENCE III	5

Field experience III is designed to introduce students to scene management, patient assessment and treatment, documentation, communication, and interaction with family and ancillary health care personnel as these skills pertain to prehospital emergency care. Emphasis is on interfacing with patients, hospitals, families, the general public, and other public service personnel. Students will finalize their field experience to total 350 clock hours from various fire department/ambulance services under the direct supervision of an approved field preceptor. This includes students serving as team leader for 120 hours. Students will demonstrate various skills outlined in the field/clinical policies.

ADVANCED CERTIFICATIONS

You may have noticed in the paramedic curriculum described above a class called "Professional Certifications." This class actually consists of four two-day courses each of which covers a separate area of specialization. Students who pass these courses earn certification in advanced cardiac life support (ACLS), pre-hospital trauma life support (PHTLS), pediatric advanced life support (PALS), and advanced medical life support (AMLS). These advanced certifications can give an EMT a competitive edge by increasing his or her chances for promotion. They are often cited on job postings for advanced positions, many of which require that applicants hold these advanced certifications or others like them.

If your training program did not include advanced certifications, you may be able to take a course or courses through a local technical or community college or even in-house if your employer is willing to provide continuing education to the staff. Other advanced certifications include basic trauma life support (BTLS), neonatal life support (NALS), and outdoor emergency care technician (OECT). Getting training above and beyond what is required will allow you to perform your job at a higher level of expertise.

JUST THE FACTS

EMS HISTORY

The first volunteer independent rescue squad in the United States was formed in 1928 in Roanoke, Virginia, by Julian Stanley Wise and nine other men. This squad was the forerunner of the modern EMS system. Wise had been committed to the idea of helping others through rescue services since he was nine years old, when he watched helplessly as two canoeists drowned in the Roanoke River. After forming the Roanoke squad, Wise dedicated his life to the further establishment of such rescue units. The Rescue Museum in Roanoke commemorates this seminal event in EMS history.

CHOOSING A TRAINING PROGRAM

Selecting the school that will best suit your needs, likes, and goals means making many decisions, including those about the type of institution (technical school, hospital, community college, or two-year college), over-all size of the school, location, and quality of programs. Would you prefer large classes held in lecture halls or smaller classes in which you get to know your professors? Do you want to go a local school and live at home, or are you willing to relocate and perhaps live in on-campus housing?

You can explore these options and many others by enlisting the help of an experienced high school guidance counselor or career counselor. If you are not currently in school, use the guidebooks listed below and the resources listed throughout this chapter to help you. And whether in school or not, you should talk with those who are already working in the emergency medical field about their experiences. Ask where they went to school, what advantages they gained from their education, and what they would do differently if they were starting again.

Training programs offered at technical or vocational schools, local hospitals, and police and fire departments vary greatly. You should expect, however, that the course will teach the national standard curriculum and prepare you to take and pass the state or national EMT-Basic exam. If this information is not specified in a school's brochure or website, ask directly. There's no point in spending the time and money on a course that doesn't teach you everything you'll need to know.

If you are interested in pursuing an EMT-Paramedic certificate through a two-year associate's degree, you might consider a community college. Community colleges are public institutions offering vocational and academic courses both during the day and at night. They cater to students who for the most part live at home and work while getting their education. They typically cost less than either two-year public or two-year private institutions. You will need a high school diploma or GED to get in, and you'll need to provide high school transcripts, recommendations, and possibly standardized test scores. You can find out the location of community colleges in your area by contacting your state's Department of Education or checking the World Wide Web through a search engine such as Yahoo.com for community colleges, which are listed by state.

JUST THE FACTS

STARTING EARLY

If you are still in high school, you may be able to receive some college credits by enrolling as a "guest student" or auditor at your local community college. Get a copy of the school's course list and pick out one or two classes you are interested in. Then contact the admissions director. Explain your career plans and interest in sitting in on a course. You'll have to pay for it, but in many cases the credit is transferable when you enter college for a degree.

Junior colleges are two-year institutions that are usually more expensive than community colleges because they tend to be privately owned. Use the Internet or the best-selling guide *Peterson's Two-Year Colleges* to help you with your search.

Another thing to consider when choosing a school is its placement programs in emergency medical services. Does it have a relationship with area hospitals and ambulance companies in which there is active recruiting on campus? Attending a school with such a relationship could greatly improve your chances of finding employment upon graduation.

ONLINE COLLEGE GUIDES

Most of these websites offer similar information, including various search methods, the ability to apply to many schools online, financial aid and scholarship information, and online test taking (PSAT, SAT, etc.). Some offer advice in selecting schools, give virtual campus tours, and help you decide what classes to take in high school. It is well worth it to visit several of them.

www.embark.com—a good general site

www.collegequest.com—run by Peterson's, a well-known publisher of college guide books (see also www.petersons.com)

www.review.com—a service of the *Princeton Review* with plenty of "insider information" on schools, custom searches for schools, and pointers on improving standardized test scores

www.collegenet.com—on the Web since 1995, the best site for applying to schools on-line

www.collegereview.com—offers good general information, plus virtual campus tours

www.theadmissionsoffice.com —answers your questions about the application process, how to improve your chances of getting accepted, and when to take tests

Visiting the Schools

Another thing you can do, if you have the time, is to visit the schools you are considering and talk to a guidance counselor or admissions officer at each one. These people are trained to help you identify your needs and decide if their school will meet those needs. Follow these steps when preparing for an on-campus visit:

▶ Contact the office of admissions to request an appointment to visit. Remember to ask for the name of the person making the appointment and the person with whom you will be meeting. Try to schedule a meeting with an instructor in the EMT program as well as a guidance counselor in the admissions or counseling department.

▶ Bring a copy of your high school transcript or permanent record card if you will have the opportunity to meet with an admissions counselor during your visit.

▶ Include a list of honors or awards you have received in high school or the community, including documentation of any EMT volunteer experience or other medical training.

▶ Ask to tour the EMT laboratories or practical experience areas, if available. This tour should show you the available equipment and materials for emergency simulations and other EMT exercises. Many schools are affiliated with one or more local hospitals, fire departments, or ambulance services, so they offer this hands-on training through another agency.

Be prepared to ask questions about the school and surrounding community, including extracurricular activities, work opportunities, and anything else you don't find explained in the promotional brochures.

ON THE JOB

Endotracheal Intubation

Endotracheal intubation is a procedure performed by EMT-Paramedics on patients who are not breathing on their own. By inserting a flexible plastic tube called an endotracheal tube through the mouth down into the trachea, the large airway from the mouth to the lungs, an open duct is created that allows air to pass through the upper airway, ventilating the lungs. The EMT inserts the tube with the help of a laryngoscope, an instrument that permits him or her to see down into the trachea and even see the vocal cords. Endotracheal tubes can be connected to ventilator machines to provide artificial respiration.

Asking the Right Questions

After you have narrowed down your choices to two or three schools, the next step is to ask tough questions about each program, to help you make the final selection. Here are some important questions you should ask about a prospective school to see if it measures up to your standards. After each question, you'll find sample answers that you should receive or other considerations that you should think about before choosing a particular school.

▶ What requirements must I meet to attend?
   Check with each school you are considering to find out what its specific entrance requirements are. Requirements vary from school to school. For instance, you may be required to do one or more of the following:

   ✓ *take English, math, or science placement tests*
   ✓ *take and achieve a certain score on the SATs or ACT if you have not already taken them in high school*
   ✓ *have a certain GPA level from high school*
   ✓ *Take a physical exam*

If one of the schools you are considering has an entrance requirement that you think you might not meet, call an admissions counselor and discuss your particular case with him or her. The school may offer some type of remedial solution so you can meet the requirement in the future.

▶ Is the program I chose accredited? If so, by whom?

It is very important that your school be accredited. Accreditation assures that the school and its programs have met high standards and compare favorably with other schools across the country. There are many agencies that accredit programs in every field of the health care industry; many of them are listed in Appendix B. Be sure the school of your choice lists one or more of them as its accrediting agency. An important point to remember is that if the school you choose is not accredited, you cannot get financial assistance through any government aid program. (See Chapter 3 for more information about how to obtain financial aid.)

▶ How much does the program cost?

You need to determine what you can afford. Find out how much tuition and application fees will cost at each school you are considering. Also ask financial aid administrators what kind of aid is available from the school. Can you receive enough financial aid to attend a large college or university? How much are tuition, books, lab fees, and tools going to cost?

The amount of money you have and the amount the training program is going to cost may determine whether you should work part-time and go to school part-time, whether you should apply for financial aid, and whether you can afford a technical institute or college.

▶ What are the faculty members' qualifications and how experienced are they?

There should be some faculty members who have advanced degrees, such as EMT-Paramedic, and many years of experience in the working world. The faculty should be accessible for student conferences.

▶ What is the student/teacher ratio?

The student/teacher ratio is a statistic that shows the average number of students assigned to one teacher in a classroom or lab. It's important that the student/teacher ratio be low enough to allow for individual attention. Education suffers if classrooms are too crowded or if a teacher has too many students to be able to see everyone who wishes to be seen for a private conference.

According to one of the top national accrediting agencies, the Accrediting Council for Independent Colleges and Schools (ACICS), a reasonable student/teacher ratio for skills training is 30 students to 1 teacher in a lecture setting and 15 students to 1 teacher in a laboratory or clinical instruction setting. At very good schools, the ratio is even better than what the ACICS recommends.

▶ What percentage of graduates of the EMT program was placed in jobs upon graduation?

The placement rate for graduates is important. A high rate may indicate that the school is committed to helping its students find employment in their chosen fields. This commitment might take the form of free placement services for the working lifetime of its graduates, on-campus recruiting, or a relationship with a local hospital or ambulance company that consistently hires new graduates.

▶ Is the school equipped with the latest EMT equipment and ambulance technology?

When you visit the school you plan to attend, ask to see the laboratory facilities and ambulance technology and equipment. The most recent and advanced computer technology and training equipment should be available to students. Some examples of the type of equipment you should look for are AEDs, heart monitors, and IV supplies.

▶ When are classes scheduled?

Find out if the school you're considering offers any weekend or evening classes. If you need to work full-time during regular business hours while attending school, you'll need to find a school that offers classes at nontraditional times.

▶ Is the campus environment suitable?

You should be able to determine this when you visit the school. Is it too big? Too small? Too quiet? Is the campus in a bustling city or a rural community? Is it easily accessible? Do you need to rely on public transportation to get there? Select a school that has a campus environment that meets your needs.

▶ Does the school offer child care facilities?

If this is a concern, you'll want to tour the child care facilities and interview the people who work there to see if the care is suitable for your children. Ask for references, and call them to speak with parents personally. You can find out if the care is satisfactory from someone who is using or has used the service.

Application Tips from Admissions Directors

✓ Apply as early as you can. You'll need to fill out an application and submit high school or GED transcripts and any copies of SAT, ACT, or other test scores used for admission. If you haven't taken these tests, you may have to do so before you can be admitted. Call the school and find out when the next program starts, then apply at least a month or two prior to that date to make sure you can complete requirements before the program begins.

✓ You may receive a prewritten request for high school transcripts from the admissions office when you get your application. Make sure you send those requests promptly, so the admissions process is not held up in any way.

✓ Make an appointment as soon as possible to take any required placement tests.

✓ Pay your fees before the deadline. Enrollment is not complete each quarter or semester until students have paid all fees by the date specified on the registration form. If fees are not paid by the deadline, their classes may be canceled. If you are going to receive financial aid, apply as early as you can.

✓ Find out early in the application process if you must pass a physical or have any other medical history forms on file for the school you choose, so this does not hold up your admission.

MAKING THE MOST OF YOUR TRAINING PROGRAM

After you accept the responsibility of entering a training program to receive a certificate or degree, you'll want to make the most of your experience. If your county or EMS company is paying for your training, you will probably have to repay it if you drop out. It is important to take your classes seriously, study hard, and take advantage of the opportunities your school offers if you want to end the program with a job offer. EMT instructor Jeanine Hoffman shares the advice she gives most often to students:

I tell them to *relax*! You don't have to go out on the street your first day and handle a situation like the World Trade Center bombing. It's a gradual learning process, and everything will fit into the schedule and build upon everything that came before it. Knowing this sometimes helps students to alleviate their fears because students tend to fear panic at certain times during the EMT course. If they read ahead, keep up with their studies, pay attention in class, and use their practical and free time wisely, they will do just fine.

INSIDE TRACK

Maxie Bishop, Jr.
Paramedic / RN / Firefighter
EMS Training Coordinator
Dallas Fire Department

When I was 28 years old and working in the oil fields in Louisiana, there were a lot of layoffs happening. One weekend I was visiting my brother, who lived across the street from a fire station in Dallas, and two of the firefighters asked me if I was interested in becoming a firefighter. That was 15 years ago, and the rest is history. Unfortunately I am currently in an office job, and the thing I dislike the most is to be stuck inside. The thing I like most about this position is being able to influence our new recruits and introduce them to the life of an EMT.

I work four days a week, Tuesday through Friday from 7 A.M. to 6 P.M. This is unusual, as most members of our department work a 24-hours-on/48-hours-off schedule. Most of my time in this position is spent doing data entry activities, making and returning telephone calls, and continuing education.

The field has changed a lot since I began. There is an increased workload; the response volume has risen an average of 10% each year. There has also been an increase in our responsibilities. Our protocol has gone from 20 to 30 pages. The skills have changed, and now we can do almost the same things as any ER [emergency room] except X-rays and sutures, and I suspect that that is coming. The biggest changes have been in the requirements for entry into the paramedic program and the classroom requirement. We have gone from not receiving any college credit to receiving 42 semester hours. I predict that there will be an associate's degree in paramedicine within the next two years.

This profession is not for everyone. You must be the type of person who is willing to give themselves and their lives to and for others. You must prepare yourself academically and physically for this job. Treatments change often and you have to stay on top of medical advancements and be willing and able to change.

CHAPTER three

BECOMING A CANDIDATE: FINANCIAL AID

THIS CHAPTER explains the three types of financial aid available: scholarships and grants, loans, and work-study programs. You'll find out how to determine your eligibility, which financial records you'll need to gather, and how to complete and file forms (a sample financial aid form is included). At the end of the chapter are listed many more resources that can help you find the aid you need.

YOU HAVE decided that you want a job as an EMT, and you've chosen a training program. Now, you need a plan for financing your training. Be assured that you can qualify for aid at several different types of schools, ranging from community colleges, technical colleges to universities, and vocational schools that offer short-term training programs, certificates, associate's degrees, and bachelor's degrees. You can often qualify for some type of financial aid even if you're attending only part-time. The financial aid you get will generally be less than in full-time programs, but it can still be worthwhile and help you pay for a portion of your EMS training program.

Don't let financial aid anxiety deter you from exploring the many options you have for financing your training program. After you've read this chapter, investigate the other resources listed in it. The Internet is probably the best source for up-to-the-minute information, and almost all of it is free. If you are in school or have been accepted to a school, take advantage of the services of financial aid advisors, whose job is to address your concerns and help you fill out the necessary paperwork.

SOME MYTHS ABOUT FINANCIAL AID

The subject of financial aid is often misunderstood. Here are three of the most common myths:

Myth #1: *All the red tape involved in finding sources and applying for financial aid is too confusing for me.*

Fact: It's really not that confusing. The whole financial aid process is a set of steps that are ordered and logical. Besides, several sources of help are available. To start, read this chapter carefully to get a helpful overview of the entire process and tips on how to get the most financial aid. Then use one or more of the resources listed within and at the end of this chapter for additional help. If you believe you'll be able to cope with college, you'll be able to cope with looking for the money to finance your education, especially if you take the process one step at a time in an organized manner.

Myth #2: *For most students, financial aid just means getting a loan and going into heavy debt, which isn't worth it, or working while in school, which will lead to burnout and poor grades.*

Fact: Both the federal government and individual schools award grants and scholarships, which the student doesn't have to pay back. It is also possible to get a combination of scholarships and loans. It's worth taking out a loan if it means attending the school you really want to attend rather than settling for your second choice or not going to school at all. As for working while in school, it's true that it is a challenge to hold down a full-time or even a part-time job while in school. However, a small amount of work-study employment (10–12 hours per week) has been shown to actually improve academic performance, because it teaches students important time-management skills.

Myth #3: *I can't understand the financial aid process because of all the unfamiliar terms and strange acronyms that are used.*

Fact: While you will encounter an amazing number of acronyms and some unfamiliar terms while applying for federal financial aid, you can refer to the acronym list and glossary at the end of this chapter for quick definitions and clear explanations of the commonly used terms and acronyms.

TYPES OF FINANCIAL AID

There are three categories of financial aid:
1. grants and scholarships—aid that you don't have to pay back
2. work/study—aid that you earn by working
3. loans—aid that you have to pay back

Grants

Grants are normally awarded based on financial need. Here are the two most common grants:

Federal Pell Grants
Federal Pell Grants are based on financial need and are awarded only to undergraduate students who have not yet earned a bachelor's or a professional degree. For many students, Pell Grants provide a foundation of financial aid to which other aid may be added. For the year 1999–2000, the maximum award was $3,125. You can receive only one Pell Grant in an award year, and you may not receive Pell Grant funds for more than one school at a time.

How much you get will depend not only on your expected family contribution (EFC) but also on your cost of attendance, whether you're a full-time or a part-time student, and whether you attend school for a full academic year or less. You can qualify for a Pell Grant even if you are enrolled only part-time in a training program. You should also be aware that some private and school-based sources of financial aid will not consider your eligibility if you haven't first applied for a Pell Grant.

Federal Supplemental Educational Opportunity Grants (FSEOGs)

FSEOGs are for undergraduates with exceptional financial need, that is, students with the lowest expected family contributions (EFC). They give priority to students who receive Pell Grants. An FSEOG is similar to a Pell Grant in that it doesn't need to be paid back.

You can receive between $100 and $4,000 a year, depending on when you apply, your level of need, and the funding level of the school you're attending. There's no guarantee that every eligible student will be able to receive an FSEOG. Students at each school are paid based on the availability of funds at that school and not all schools participate in this program. To have the best chances of getting this grant, apply as early as you can after January 1 of the year in which you plan to attend school.

IN THE NEWS

The Future of EMS

According to the *EMS Agenda for the Future*, published by the National Highway Traffic Safety Administration (NHTSA), the federal agency that oversees the nations's EMS programs, the future of EMS will have more of a focus on "community-based health management that is fully integrated with the overall health care system . . . [while] remaining the public's emergency medical safety net."

Scholarships

Scholarships can be awarded for academic merit or for special characteristics (for example, ethnic heritage, interests, sports, parents' career, college major, or geographic location) as well as financial need. As with grants, you do not pay your award money back. Scholarships may be offered from federal, state, school, and private sources.

The best way to find scholarship money is to use one of the free search tools available on the Internet. After entering the appropriate information about yourself, a search takes place which ends with a list of those prizes for which you are eligible. Try www.fastasp.org, which bills itself as the world's largest and oldest private-sector scholarship database; www.college-scholarships.com and www.gripvision.com are also good sites for conducting searches. If you don't have easy access to the Internet or want to expand your search, high school guidance counselors or college financial aid officers also have plenty of information about available scholarship money.

To find private sources of aid, spend a few hours in the library looking at scholarship and fellowship books, or consider a reasonably priced (under $30) scholarship search service. See the resources section at the end of this chapter to find contact information for search services and scholarship book titles. Use caution when dealing with scholarship search services. While most are perfectly legitimate, some scams have been reported. If you're unsure, contact a financial aid officer. Another place to check is in EMS magazines. If you're currently employed, find out if your employer has educational funds available. If you're a dependent student, ask your parents and other relatives to check with groups or organizations they belong to for possible aid sources. Consider these popular sources of scholarship money:

- ► religious organizations
- ► fraternal organizations
- ► clubs, such as the Rotary, Kiwanis, American Legion, or 4H
- ► athletic clubs
- ► veterans' groups
- ► ethnic group associations
- ► unions

If you already know which school you will attend, check with a financial aid administrator (FAA) in the financial aid department to find out if you qualify for any school-based scholarships or other aid. Many schools offer merit-based aid for students with a high school GPA of a certain level or with a certain level of SAT scores, in order to attract more students. Check with the department that offers EMT courses to see if it maintains a bulletin board or other method of posting available scholarships that are specific to EMS programs.

While you are looking for sources of scholarships, continue to enhance your chances of winning one by participating in extracurricular events and volunteer activities. You should also obtain references from people who know you well and are leaders in the community, so you can submit their names and/or letters with your scholarship applications. Make a list of any awards you've received in the past or other honors that you could list on your scholarship application.

EMS Scholarships

There are thousands of scholarships awarded to students planning to enter the prehospital care community. Below are two examples. More information about these scholarships may be found at www.umuc.edu/studserv/fineaid.html. To find more sources, search the Internet with terms such as "emergency medical services" and "scholarships."

Yvorra Leadership Development Scholarship Foundation

The Yvorra Leadership Development Foundation offers scholarships to members of emergency service organizations. These include volunteer, part-paid, and career personnel from rescue squads and emergency medical services. Contact the foundation at PO Box 408, Port Republic, MD 20676 or call 410-586-3048 for more information.

Maryland State Scholarship Administration

Maryland residents who are pursuing a degree in the EMS field who agree to serve in Maryland as rescue squad members for a certain amount of time after graduation may be eligible for a scholarship from the Maryland State Higher Education Commission. Contact the commission at 16 Francis Street, Annapolis, MD 21401 for more information.

A program that benefits mainly middle-class students is the Hope Scholarship Credit. Eligible taxpayers may claim a credit for tuition and fees up to a maximum of $1,500 per student (the amount is scheduled to be reindexed for inflation after 2001). The credit applies only to the first two years of postsecondary education, and students must be enrolled at least half-time. Families whose adjusted gross income is $80,000 or more are ineligible. To find out more about the Hope Scholarship credit, log onto www.sfas.com.

Work-Study Programs

When applying to a college or university, you can indicate that you are interested in a work-study program. You'll then be given the details about the types of jobs offered under various programs (they can range from giving tours of the campus to prospective students to working in the cafeteria or shelving library books) and how much they pay.

There is also the possibility of getting money for college by first securing a job with an ambulance company that agrees to pay all or part of your educational expenses. Some will pay only for classes related to the job, either as defined in a detailed formal policy or as you may have to get your classes approved on a case-by-case basis. Some departments make it even easier to attend college by permitting supervisors to adjust your work shifts and schedules so that you can attend classes. Others offer financial incentives not only for college classes, but also for advanced state certification courses and certain in-service training programs.

JUST THE FACTS

Firefighter-EMTs

More than 95% of EMS aid provided at fires is furnished by firefighter-EMTs. This represents an important aspect of the future of both professions, as increasing emphasis is put on dual role fulfillment.

You may also want to investigate the Federal Work-Study (FWS) program, which can be applied for through the FAFSA (Free Application for Federal Student Aid). The FWS program provides jobs for undergraduate and graduate students with financial need, allowing them to earn money to help pay educational expenses. It encourages community service work and provides hands-on experience related to your course of study when available. The amount of the FWS award depends on

▶ when you apply (again, apply early)
▶ your level of need
▶ the funds available at your particular school

FSW salaries are the current federal minimum wage or higher, depending on the type of work and skills required. As an undergraduate, you'll be paid by the hour (a graduate student may receive a salary), and you will receive the money directly from your school; you cannot be paid by commission or fee. The awards are not transferable from year to year, and you will need to check with the schools to which you're applying; not all schools have work-study programs in every area of study.

An advantage of working under the FWS program is that your earnings are exempt from FICA (Federal Insurance Contributions Act) taxes if you are enrolled full-time and are working less than half-time. You will be assigned a job on campus, in a private nonprofit organization, or with a public agency that offers a public service. You may provide a community service relating to emergency services if your school has such a program. Some schools have agreements with private for-profit companies if the work demands your emergency skills. The total hourly wages you earn in each year cannot exceed your total FWS award for that year, and you cannot work more than 20 hours per week. Your FAA or the direct employer must consider your class schedule and your academic progress before assigning a job.

Student Loans

Although scholarships, grants, and even work-study programs can help to offset the costs of higher education, they usually don't give you enough money to pay your way entirely. Most students who can't afford to pay for their entire education rely at least in part on student loans. The largest single source for these loans—and for all money for students—is the federal government. Try these three sites for information about the U.S. government programs:

www.fedmoney.org
> This site explains everything from the application process (you can actually download the applications you'll need) and eligibility requirements to the different types of loans available.

www.finaid.org
> Here you can find a calculator for figuring out how much money your education will cost (and how much you'll need to borrow), instructions for filling out the necessary forms, and even information on the various types of military aid.

www.ed.gov/offices/OSFAP/students
> This is the federal student financial aid home page. The FAFSA can be filled out and submitted on-line.

You can also get excellent detailed information about different sources of federal education funding by sending away for a copy of the U.S. Department of Education's free publication *The Student Guide*. Write to:

Federal Student Aid Information Center
PO Box 84
Washington, DC 20044
1-800-4-FED-AID

Below are listed some of the most popular federal loan programs:

Federal Perkins Loans A Perkins Loan has the lowest interest (currently 5%) of any loan available for both undergraduate and graduate students and is offered to students with exceptional financial need. You repay your school, which lends the money to you with government funds.

Depending on when you apply, your level of need, and the funding level of the school, you can borrow up to $4,000 for each year of undergraduate study. The total amount you can borrow as an undergraduate is $20,000.

The school pays you directly by check or credits your tuition account. You have nine months after you graduate (provided you were continuously enrolled at least half-time) to begin repayment, with up to 10 years to pay off the entire loan.

PLUS Loans (Parent Loans for Undergraduate Students) These loans enable parents with good credit histories to borrow money to pay the educational expenses of a child who is a dependent undergraduate student enrolled at least half-time. Your parents must submit the completed forms to your school.

To be eligible, your parents will be required to pass a credit check. If they don't pass, they might still be able to receive a loan if they can show that extenuating circumstances exist or if someone who is able to pass the credit check agrees to co-sign the loan. Your parents must also meet citizenship requirements.

The yearly limit on a PLUS Loan is equal to your cost of attendance minus any other financial aid you receive. For instance, if your cost of attendance is $6,000 and you receive $4,000 in other financial aid, your parents could borrow up to, but no more than, $2,000. The interest rate varies, but is not to exceed 9% over the life of the loan. Your parents must begin repayment while you're still in school. There is no grace period.

Federal Stafford Loans Stafford Loans are low-interest loans that are given to students who attend school at least half-time. The maximum amount you can borrow is $23,000 as a dependent undergraduate student. The lender is the U.S. Department of Education or a bank you select, depending on the loan program under which you borrow. Check with your financial aid office for details. Stafford Loans fall into one of two categories:

▶ Subsidized loans are awarded on the basis of financial need. You will not be charged any interest before you begin repayment or during authorized periods of deferment. The federal government subsidizes the interest during these periods.
▶ Unsubsidized loans are not awarded on the basis of financial need. You'll be charged interest from the time the loan is disbursed until it is paid in full. If you allow the interest to accumulate, it will be capitalized, that is, the interest will be added to the principal amount of your loan, and additional interest will be based upon the higher amount. This will increase the amount you have to repay.

There are many borrowing limit categories to these loans, depending on whether you get an unsubsidized or a subsidized loan, which year in school you're enrolled, how long your program of study is, and whether you're independent or dependent. You can have both kinds of Stafford Loans at the same time; your financial aid office will certify your eligibility for both programs, which varies. The interest rate varies, but should not exceed 8.25%. An origination fee for a Stafford Loan is approximately 3 or 4% of the loan, and the fee will be deducted from each loan disbursement you receive. There is a six-month grace period after graduation before you must start repaying the loan.

Loan money is also available from state governments. Following is a list of the agencies responsible for giving out such loans, with websites and e-mail addresses where available.

ALABAMA

Alabama Commission on Higher Education

100 North Union Street

PO Box 302000

Montgomery, AL 36130-2000

334-242-2276

ALASKA

Alaska Commission on Postsecondary

 Education

3030 Vintage Boulevard

Juneau, AK 99801-7109

907-465-6741

Fax: 907-465-5316

ARIZONA

Arizona Commission for Postsecondary

 Education

2020 North Central Avenue, Suite 275

Phoenix, AZ 85004-4503

602-229-2591

Fax: 602-229-2599

Website: www.acpe.asu.edu

ARKANSAS

Arkansas Department of Education

4 State Capitol Mall, Room 107A

Little Rock, AR 72201-1071

501-682-4396

E-mail: finaid@adhe.arknet.edu

CALIFORNIA

California Student Aid Commission

PO Box 419026

Rancho Cordova, CA 95741-9026

Customer Service Department: 916-526-

 7590

Fax: 916-323-2619

COLORADO

Colorado Commission on Higher Education

Colorado Heritage Center

1300 Broadway, 2nd Floor

Denver, CO 80203

303-866-2723

Fax: 303-860-9750

CONNECTICUT

Connecticut Department of Higher

 Education

61 Woodland Street

Hartford, CT 06105-2326

860-947-1855

Fax: 860-947-1311

DELAWARE

Delaware Higher Education Commission

Carvel State Office Building, 4th Floor

820 North French Street

Wilmington, DE 19801

302-577-3240

Fax: 302-577-6765

DISTRICT OF COLUMBIA

Department of Human Services

Office of Postsecondary Education

Research and Assistance

2100 Martin Luther King Jr. Avenue SE,
    Suite 401

Washington, DC 20020

202-727-3688

Fax: 202-727-2739

FLORIDA

Florida Department of Education

Office of Student Financial Assistance

1344 Florida Education Center

325 West Gaines Street

Tallahassee, FL 32399-0400

888-827-2004

Fax: 850-488-3612

GEORGIA

Georgia Student Finance Commission

2082 East Exchange Place, Suite 100

Tucker, GA 30084

770-724-9030

Website: www.gsfc.org

HAWAII

Hawaii State Postsecondary Education
    Commission

2444 Dole Street, Room 209

Honolulu, HI 96822-2394

808-956-8207

Fax: 808-956-5156

IDAHO

Idaho State Board of Education

PO Box 83720

Boise, ID 83720-0037

208-334-2270

Fax: 208-334-2632

ILLINOIS

Illinois Student Assistance Commission
    (ISAC)

1755 Lake Cook Road

Deerfield, IL 60015-5209

800-899-4722

Website: www.isac-online.org

INDIANA

State Student Assistance Commission of
    Indiana

150 West Market Street, Suite 500

Indianapolis, IN 46204-2811

317-232-2350

Fax: 317-232-3260

IOWA

Iowa College Student Aid Commission

200 10th Street, 4th Floor

Des Moines, Iowa 50309-3609

515-281-3501

E-mail: csac@max.state.ia.us

Website: www.iowacollegeaid.org

KANSAS

Kansas Board of Regents

700 SW Harrison, Suite 1410

Topeka, KS 66603-3760

785-296-3517

Fax: 785-296-0983

E-mail: christy@kbor.state.ks.us

Website: www.ukans.edu/~kbor

KENTUCKY

Kentucky Higher Education Assistance

Authority (KHEAA)

1050 U.S. 127 South

Frankfort, KY 40601-4323

800-928-8926

Fax: 502-696-7345

E-mail: webmaster@kheaa.com

Website: www.kheaa.com

LOUISIANA

Louisiana Office of Student Financial

Assistance

PO Box 91202

Baton Rouge, LA 70821-9202

800-259-5626, ext. 1012

225-922-1012

Fax: 225-922-1089

E-mail for students:

custserv@osfa.state.la.us or

webmaster@osfa.state.la.us

Website: www.osfa.state.la.us

MAINE

Finance Authority of Maine

PO Box 949

Augusta, ME 04332-0949

800-228-3734

207-623-3263

Fax: 207-626-8208

TDD: 207-626-2717

E-mail: info@famemaine.com

MARYLAND

Maryland Higher Education Commission

Jeffrey Building, 16 Francis Street

Annapolis, MD 21401-1781

410-974-5370

Fax: 410-974-5994

MASSACHUSETTS

Massachusetts Board of Higher Education

Office of Student Financial Assistance

330 Stuart Street, 3rd Floor

Boston, MA 02116

617-727-1205

Fax: 617-727-0667

MICHIGAN

Michigan Higher Education Assistance

Authority

Office of Scholarships and Grants

PO Box 30462

Lansing, MI 48909-7962

517-373-3394

Fax: 517-335-5984

MINNESOTA

Minnesota Higher Education Services Office

1450 Energy Park Drive, Suite 350

Street Paul, MN 55108-5227

800-657-3866

651-642-0567

Website: www.mheso.state.mn.us

MISSISSIPPI

Mississippi Postsecondary Education

Financial Assistance Board

3825 Ridgewood Road

Jackson, MS 39211-6453

601-982-6663

Fax: 601-982-6527

MISSOURI

Missouri Student Assistance Resource

Services (MOSTARS)

3515 Amazonas Drive

Jefferson City, MO 65109-5717

800-473-6757

573-751-3940

Fax: 573-751-6635

Website: www.mocbhe.gov/mostars/

finmenu.htm

MONTANA

Office of Commissioner of Higher Education

Montana Guaranteed Student Loan Program

PO Box 203101

Helena, MT 59620-3101

800-537-7508

E-mail: scholars@mgslp.state.mt.us

Website: www.mgslp.state.mt.us

NEBRASKA

Coordinating Commission for Postsecondary

Education

PO Box 95005

Lincoln, NE 68509-5005

402-471-2847

Fax: 402-471-2886

Website:

www.ccpe.state.ne.us/PublicDoc/CCPE/

Default.asp

NEVADA

Nevada Department of Education

700 East Fifth Street

Carson City, NV 89701-5096

775-687-9200

Fax: 775-687-9101

NEW HAMPSHIRE

Postsecondary Education Commission

2 Industrial Park Drive

Concord, NH 03301-8512

603-271-2555

Fax: 603-271-2696

E-mail: jknapp@nhsa.state.nh.us

Website: www.state.nh.us

NEW JERSEY

Higher Education Student Assistance

Authority

PO Box 540

Trenton, NJ 08625

800-792-8670

Fax: 609-588-3316

Website: www.state.nj.us/treasury/osa

NEW MEXICO

New Mexico Commission on Higher
    Education
1068 Cerrillos Road
Santa Fe, NM 87501
800-279-9777
E-mail: highered@che.state.nm.us
Website: www.nmche.org

NEW YORK

New York State Higher Education Services
    Corporation
One Commerce Plaza
Albany, NY 12255
888-697-4372
Fax: 518-473-3749

NORTH CAROLINA

North Carolina State Education Assistance
    Authority
PO Box 13663
Research Triangle Park, NC 27709-3663
800-700-1775
E-mail: information@ncseaa.edu

NORTH DAKOTA

North Dakota University System
North Dakota Student Financial Assistance
    Program
600 East Boulevard Avenue, Dept. 215
Bismarck, ND 58505-0230
701-328-4114
Fax: 701-328-2961

OHIO

Ohio Board of Regents
PO Box 182452
Columbus, OH 43218-2452
888-833-1133
Fax: 614-752-5903

OKLAHOMA

Oklahoma State Regents for Higher
    Education
500 Education Building
Oklahoma City, OK 73105-4503
405-858-4356
Fax: 405-858-4577

OREGON

Oregon State Scholarship Commission
1500 Valley River Drive, Suite 100
Eugene, OR 97401-2130
800-452-8807
Fax: 541-687-7419
Website: www.ossc.state.or.us

PENNSYLVANIA

Pennsylvania Higher Education Assistance
    Authority
1200 North Seventh Street
Harrisburg, PA 17102-1444
800-692-7435
Website: www.pheaa.org

RHODE ISLAND

Rhode Island Higher Education Assistance
    Authority
560 Jefferson Boulevard
Warwick, Rhode Island 02886
401-736-1170
Fax: 401-736-3541
TDD: 401-222-6195

SOUTH CAROLINA

South Carolina Higher Education Tuition
    Grants Commission
PO Box 12159
Columbia, SC 29211
803-734-1200
Fax: 803-734-1426
Website: www.state.sc.us/tuitiongrants

SOUTH DAKOTA

Department of Education and Cultural Affairs
Office of the Secretary
700 Governors Drive
Pierre, SD 57501-2291
605-773-3134
Fax: 605-773-6139

TENNESSEE

Tennessee Student Assistance Corporation
404 James Robertson Parkway, Suite 1950
Nashville, TN 37243
800-342-1663
615-741-1346
Fax: 615-741-6101
Website: www.state.tn.us/tsac

TEXAS

Texas Higher Education Coordinating Board
PO Box 12788, Capitol Station
Austin, TX 78711
800-242-3062
Fax: 512-427-6420

UTAH

Utah State Board of Regents
Utah System of Higher Education
355 West North Temple
#3 Triad Center, Suite 550
Salt Lake City, UT 84180-1205
801-321-7200
Fax: 801-321-7299

VERMONT

Vermont Student Assistance Corporation
PO Box 2000
Winooski, VT 05404-2601
800-642-3177
800-655-9602
Fax: 800-654-3765
E-mail: info@vsac.org
Website: www.vsac.org

VIRGINIA

State Council of Higher Education for
    Virginia
James Monroe Building
101 North Fourteenth Street
Richmond, VA 23219-3684
804-786-1690
Fax: 804-225-2604

WASHINGTON

Washington State Higher Education
 Coordinating Board
PO Box 43430
917 Lakeridge Way
Olympia, WA 98501-3430
360-753-7850
Fax: 360-753-7808
E-mail: info@hecb.wa.gov
Website: www.hecb.wa.gov

WEST VIRGINIA

State College & University Systems of West
 Virginia Central Office
1018 Kanawha Boulevard East, Suite 700
Charleston, WV 25301-2827
304-558-4016
Fax: 304-558-0259

WISCONSIN

Higher Educational Aids Board
PO Box 7885
Madison, WI 53707-7885
608-267-2944
Fax: 608-267-2808
Website: http://heab.state.wi.us

WYOMING

Wyoming Community College Commission
2020 Carey Avenue, 8th Floor
Cheyenne, WY 82002
307-777-7763
Fax: 307-777-6567

Questions to Ask before You Take Out a Loan

In order to get the facts regarding the loan you're about to take out, ask the following questions:

1. What is the interest rate and how often is the interest capitalized? Your college's financial aid administrator will be able to tell you this.

2. What fees will be charged? Government loans generally have an origination fee that goes to the federal government to help offset its costs, and a guarantee fee, which goes to a guaranty agency for insuring the loan. Both are deducted from the amount given to you.

3. Will I have to make any payments while still in school? Usually you won't and, depending on the type of loan, the government may even pay the interest for you while you're in school.

4. What is the grace period, the period after my schooling ends, during which no payment is required? Is the grace period long enough, realistically, for you to find a job and get on your feet? (A six-month grace period is common.)

5. When will my first payment be due and approximately how much will it be? You can get a good preview of the repayment process from the answer to this question.

6. Who exactly will hold my loan? To whom will I be sending payments? Whom should I contact with questions or inform of changes in my situation? Your loan may be sold by the original lender to a secondary market institution, in which case you will be notified as to the contact information for your new lender.

7. Will I have the right to prepay the loan, without penalty, at any time? Some loan programs allow prepayment with no penalty but others do not.

8. Will deferments and forbearances be possible if I am temporarily unable to make payments? You need to find out how to apply for a deferment or forbearance if you need it.

9. Will the loan be canceled, or forgiven, if I become totally and permanently disabled or if I die? This is always a good option to have on any loan you take out.

APPLYING FOR FINANCIAL AID

Now that you're aware of the types of aid available, you'll want to begin applying as soon as possible. You've heard about the Free Application for Federal Student Aid (FAFSA) many times in this chapter already, and have an idea of its importance. This is the form used by federal and state governments, as well as school and private funding sources, to determine your eligibility for grants, scholarships, and loans. The easiest way to get a copy is to log onto www.ed.gov/offices/OSFAP/students, where you can find help in completing the FAFSA, and then submit the form electronically when you are finished. You can also get a copy by calling 800-4-FED-AID or stopping by your public library or your school's financial aid office. Be sure to get an original form, because photocopies of federal forms are not accepted.

The second step in the process is to create a financial aid calendar. Using any standard calendar, write in all of the application deadlines for each step of the financial aid process. This way, all vital information will be in one location, so you can see at a glance what needs to be done when. Start this calendar by writing in the date you requested your FAFSA. Then mark down when you received it and when you sent in the completed form. Add important dates and deadlines for any other applications you need to complete for school-based or private aid as you progress though the financial aid process. Using and maintaining a calendar will help the whole financial aid process run more smoothly and give you peace of mind that the important dates are not forgotten.

When to Apply

Apply for financial aid as soon as possible after January 1 of the year in which you want to enroll in school. For example, if you want to begin school in the fall of 2001, then you should apply for financial aid as soon as possible after January 1, 2001. It is easier to complete the FAFSA after you have completed your tax return, so you may want to consider filing your taxes as early as possible as well. Do not sign, date, or send your application before January 1 of the year for which you are seeking aid. If you apply by mail, send your completed application in the envelope that came with the original application. The envelope is already addressed, and using it will make sure your application reaches the correct address. Do not send the FAFSA by FedEx, UPS, or other overnight mail, as it will not get there (the FAFSA is sent to a post office box).

Many students lose out on thousands of dollars in grants and loans because they file too late. A financial aid administrator from New Jersey says:

> When you fill out the Free Application for Federal Student Aid (FAFSA), you are applying for all aid available, both federal and state, work-study, student loans, etc. The important thing is complying with the deadline date. Those students who do are considered for the Pell Grant, the SEOG (Supplemental Educational Opportunity Grant) and the Perkins Loan, which is the best loan as far as interest goes. Lots of students miss the June 30th deadline, and it can mean losing $2,480 from TAG, about $350 from WPCNJ, and another $1,100 from EOF. Students, usually the ones who need the money most, often ignore the deadlines.

After you mail in your completed FAFSA, your application will be processed in approximately four weeks. Then, you will receive a Student

Aid Report (SAR) in the mail. The SAR will disclose your Expected Family Contribution (EFC), the number used to determine your eligibility for federal student aid. Each school you list on the application may also receive your application information if the school is set up to receive it electronically.

You must reapply for financial aid every year. However, after your first year, you will receive a Student Aid Report (SAR) in the mail before the application deadline. If no corrections need to be made, you can just sign it and send it in.

Getting Your Forms Filed

Follow these three simple steps if you are not completing and submitting the FAFSA online:

1. Get an original FAFSA. Remember to pick up an original copy of this form, as photocopies are not acceptable.
2. Fill out the entire FAFSA as completely as possible. Make an appointment with a financial aid counselor if you need help. Read the forms completely, and don't skip any relevant portions.
3. Return the FAFSA before the deadline date. Financial aid counselors warn that many students don't file the forms before the deadline and lose out on available aid. Don't be one of those students!

Financial Need

Financial aid from many of the programs discussed in this chapter is awarded on the basis of need (the exceptions include unsubsidized Stafford, PLUS, and consolidation loans and some scholarships and grants). When you apply for federal student aid by completing the FAFSA, the information you report is used in a formula established by the U.S. Congress. The formula determines your Expected Family Contribution (EFC), the amount you and your family are expected to contribute toward your education. If your EFC is below a certain amount, you'll be eligible for a Pell Grant, assuming you meet all other eligibility requirements.

There is no maximum EFC that defines eligibility for the other financial aid options. Instead, your EFC is used in an equation to determine your financial needs.

Cost of Attendance − EFC = Financial Need

A financial aid administrator calculates your cost of attendance and subtracts the amount you and your family are expected to contribute toward that cost. If there's anything left over, you're considered to have financial need.

Are You Considered Dependent or Independent?

Federal policy uses strict and specific criteria to make this designation, and those criteria apply to all applicants for federal student aid equally. A dependent student is expected to have parental contribution to school expenses; an independent student is not. The parental contribution depends on the number of parents with earned income, their income and assets, the age of the older parent, the family size, and the number of family members enrolled in postsecondary education. Income is not just the adjusted gross income from the tax return, but also includes nontaxable income such as social security benefits and child support.

You're an independent student if at least one of the following applies to you:

▶ you are 26 years old before January 1 of the year in which you apply
▶ you're married (even if you're separated)
▶ you have legal dependents other than a spouse who get more than half of their support from you and will continue to get that support during the award year
▶ you're an orphan or a ward of the court (or were a ward of the court until age 18)
▶ you're a graduate or professional student
▶ you're a veteran of the U.S. Armed Forces—formerly engaged in active service in the U.S. Army, Navy, Air Force, Marines, or Coast

Guard or as a cadet or midshipman at one of the service academies—released under a condition other than dishonorable. (ROTC students, members of the National Guard, and most reservists are not considered veterans, nor are cadets and midshipmen still enrolled in one of the military service academies.)

If you live with your parents and if they claimed you as a dependent on their last tax return, then your need will be based on your parents' income. You do not qualify for independent status just because your parents have decided to not claim you as an exemption on their tax return (this used to be the case but is no longer) or do not want to provide financial support for your college education.

Students are classified as dependent or independent because federal student aid programs are based on the idea that students (and their parents or spouse, if applicable) have the primary responsibility for paying for their postsecondary (that is, after high school) education.

Gathering Financial Records

Your financial need for most grants and loans depends on your financial situation. Now that you've determined whether you are considered a dependent or an independent student, you'll know whose financial records you need to gather for this step of the process. If you are a dependent student, then you must gather not only your own financial records, but also those of your parents, because you must report their income and assets as well as your own when you complete the FAFSA. If you are an independent student, then you need to gather only your own financial records (and those of your spouse if you're married). Gather your tax records from the year prior to the one in which you are applying. For example, if you apply for the fall of 2001, you will use your tax records from 2000.

To help you fill out the FAFSA, gather the following documents:

- U.S. income tax returns (IRS Form 1040, 1040A, or 1040EZ) for the year that just ended and W-2 and 1099 forms

- records of untaxed income, such as Social Security benefits, AFDC (Aid to Families with Dependent Children), ADC (Aid to Dependent Children), child support, welfare, pensions, military subsistence allowances, and veterans' benefits
- current bank statements and mortgage information
- medical and dental expenses for the past year that weren't covered by health insurance
- business and/or farm records
- records of investments, such as stocks, bonds, and mutual funds, as well as bank Certificates of Deposit (CDs) and recent statements from money market accounts
- Social Security number(s)

Even if you do not complete your federal income tax return until March or April, you should not wait to file your FAFSA until your tax returns are filed with the IRS. Instead, use estimated income information and submit the FAFSA, as noted earlier, just as soon as possible after January 1. Be as accurate as possible, knowing that you can correct estimates later.

GENERAL GUIDELINES FOR LOANS

Before you commit yourself to any loans, be sure to keep in mind that they need to be repaid. Estimate realistically how much you'll earn when you leave school, remembering that you'll have other monthly obligations, such as housing, food, and transportation expenses.

Once You're in School

Once you have your loan (or loans) and you're attending classes, don't forget about your responsibility for your loan. Keep a file of information on your loan that includes copies of all your loan documents and related correspondence, along with a record of all your payments. Open and read all your mail about your educational loan. Make sure mail about your loans and other financial aid paperwork is forwarded *promptly* if you are temporarily staying at a different address.

Remember also that you are obligated by law to notify both your financial aid administrator and the holder or servicer of your loan if there is a change in your:

▶ name
▶ address
▶ enrollment status (dropping to less than half-time means that you'll have to begin payment six months later)
▶ anticipated graduation date

After You Leave School

After graduation, you must begin repaying your student loan either immediately or after a grace period. For example, if you have a Stafford Loan, you will be provided with a six-month grace period before your first payment is due; other types of loans have grace periods as well. If you haven't been out in the world of work before, with your loan repayment you'll begin your credit history. If you make payments on time, you'll build up a good credit rating, and credit will be easier for you to obtain for other things. Get off to a good start, so you don't run the risk of going into default. If you default, or refuse to pay back your loan, any number of things could happen to you as a result. You could

▶ have trouble getting any kind of credit in the future
▶ no longer qualify for federal or state educational financial aid
▶ have holds placed on your college records
▶ have your wages garnished
▶ have future federal income tax refunds withheld
▶ have your assets seized

To avoid the negative consequences of going into default on your loan, be sure to do the following:

▶ Open and read all mail you receive about your educational loans immediately.

► Make scheduled payments on time; since interest is calculated daily, delays can be costly.

► Contact your servicer immediately if you can't make payments on time; he or she may be able to get you into a graduated or income-sensitive/income-contingent repayment plan or work with you to arrange a deferment or forbearance.

There are a few circumstances under which you won't have to repay your loan. If you become permanently and totally disabled, you probably will not have to do so (providing the disability did not exist prior to your obtaining the aid). The same holds true if you die, if your school closes permanently in the middle of the term, or if you are erroneously certified for aid by the financial aid office; however, if you're simply disappointed in your program of study or don't get the job you wanted after graduation, you are not relieved of your obligation.

Loan Repayment

When it comes time to repay your loan, you will make payments to your original lender, to a secondary market institution to which your lender has sold your loan, or to a loan servicing specialist acting as its agent to collect payments. At the beginning of the process, try to choose the lender that offers you the best benefits (for example, a lender that lets you pay electronically, offers lower interest rates to those who consistently pay on time, or who has a toll-free number to call 24 hours a day, seven days a week). Ask the financial aid administrator at your college to direct you to such lenders.

Be sure to check out your repayment options before borrowing. Lenders are required to offer repayment plans that will make it easier to pay back your loans. Your repayment options may include:

► Standard repayment, with full principal and interest payments due each month throughout your loan term.

You'll pay the least amount of total interest using the standard repayment plan, but your monthly payments may seem high when you're just out of school.

▶ Graduated repayment where only interest or partial-interest monthly payments are due early in repayment and the payment amounts increase thereafter. Such interest-only or partial-interest repayment options offered by some lenders provide the lowest initial monthly payments available.

▶ Income-based repayment, in which monthly payments are based on a percentage of your monthly income.

▶ A consolidation loan, which allows the borrower to consolidate several types of federal student loans with various repayment schedules into one loan.

This loan is designed to help student or parent borrowers simplify their loan repayments. The interest rate on a consolidation loan may be lower than what you're currently paying on one or more of your loans. The phone number for loan consolidation at the William D. Ford Direct Loan Program is 800-557-7392. Financial administrators recommend that you do not consolidate a Perkins Loan with any other loans, since the interest on a Perkins Loan is already the lowest available. Loan consolidation is not available from all lenders.

▶ Prepayment, or paying more than is required on your loan each month or in a lump sum. This option is allowed for all federally sponsored loans at any time during the life of the loan without penalty. Prepayment will reduce the total cost of your loan.

It's quite possible—in fact likely—that while you're still in school your FFELP (Federal Family Education Loan Program) loan will be sold to a secondary market institution such as Sallie Mae. You'll be notified of the sale by letter, and you need not worry if this happens. Your loan terms and conditions will remain exactly the same; they may even improve. Indeed, the sale may give you repayment options and benefits that you would not have had otherwise. Your payments after you finish school and your requests for information should be directed to the new loan holder.

If you receive any interest-bearing student loans after graduation, you will have to attend exit counseling, where the loan lenders will tell you the total amount of debt and work out a payment schedule with you to determine the amount and dates of repayment. Many loans do not become due until at least six to nine months after you graduate, giving you a grace period. For example, you do not have to begin paying on the Perkins Loan until nine months after you graduate. This grace period is to give you time to find a good job and start earning money. However, during this time you may have to pay the interest on your loan.

If for some reason you remain unemployed when your payments become due, you may receive an unemployment deferment for a certain length of time. For many loans, you will have a maximum repayment period of 10 years (excluding periods of deferment and forbearance).

THE MOST FREQUENTLY ASKED QUESTIONS ABOUT FINANCIAL AID

Here are answers to the most frequently asked questions about student financial aid:

1. *I probably don't qualify for aid. Should I apply for it anyway?* Yes. Many students and families mistakenly think they don't qualify for aid and fail to apply. Remember that there are some sources of aid that are not based on need. The FAFSA form is free; there's no good reason for not applying.

2. *Do I need to be admitted to a particular university before I can apply for financial aid?* No. You can apply for financial aid any time after January 1. However, to get the funds, you must be admitted and enrolled in school.

3. *Do I have to reapply for financial aid every year?* Yes, and if your financial circumstances change, you may get either more or less aid. After your first year, you will receive a renewal application that contains preprinted information from the previous year's FAFSA. Renewal of your aid also depends on your making satisfactory progress toward a degree and achieving a minimum GPA.

4. *Are my parents responsible for my educational loans?* No. You and you alone are responsible unless they endorse or co-sign your loan. Parents are, however, responsible for the federal PLUS loans. If your parents (or grandparents or uncle or distant cousins) want to help pay off your loan, you can have your billing statements sent to their address.

5. *If I take a leave of absence from school, do I have to start repaying my loans?* Not immediately, but you will after the grace period. Generally, though, if you use your grace period up during your leave, you'll have to begin repayment immediately after graduation unless you apply for an extension of the grace period before it's used up.

6. *If I get assistance from another source, should I report it to the student financial aid office?* Yes, and, sadly, your aid amount may be lowered accordingly. But you'll get into trouble later on if you don't report it.

7. *Are federal work-study earnings taxable?* Yes, you must pay federal and state income tax on them, although you may be exempt from FICA taxes if you are enrolled full-time and work less than 20 hours a week.

8. *My parents are separated or divorced. Which parent is responsible for filling out the FAFSA?* If your parents are separated or divorced, the custodial parent is responsible for filling out the FAFSA. The custodial parent is the parent with whom you lived the most during the past 12 months. Note that this is not necessarily the same as the parent who has legal custody. The question of which parent must fill out the FAFSA becomes complicated in many situations, so you should take your particular circumstances to the student financial aid office for help.

Financial Aid Checklist

❏ Explore your options as soon as possible once you've decided to begin a training program.

❏ Find out what your school requires and what financial aid it offers.

❏ Complete and mail the FAFSA as soon as possible after January 1.

❏ Complete and mail other applications by their deadlines.

❏ Return all requested paperwork promptly to the financial aid office.

❏ Gather loan application information and forms from your college financial aid office.

❏ Send your completed loan application to your financial aid office for processing. Be sure to sign your loan application.

❏ Carefully read all letters and notices from the school, the federal student aid processor, the need analysis service, and private scholarship organizations. Note whether financial aid will be sent before or after you are notified about admission and how exactly you will receive the money.

❏ Report any changes in your financial resources or expenses to your financial aid office so your award can be adjusted accordingly.

❏ Reapply each year.

Financial Aid Acronyms Key

COA	Cost of Attendance
CWS	College Work-Study
EFC	Expected Family Contribution
EFT	Electronic Funds Transfer
ESAR	Electronic Student Aid Report
ETS	Educational Testing Service
FAA	Financial Aid Administrator
FAF	Financial Aid Form
FAFSA	Free Application for Federal Student Aid
FAO	Financial Aid Office
FDSLP	Federal Direct Student Loan Program
FFELP	Federal Family Education Loan Program
FSEOG	Federal Supplemental Educational Opportunity Grant
FWS	Federal Work-Study
GSL	Guaranteed Student Loan (former name of the subsidized Stafford Loan)
PC	Parent Contribution
PLUS	Parent Loan for Undergraduate Students
SAP	Satisfactory Academic Progress
SC	Student Contribution
SLS	Supplemental Loan for Students (former name of the unsubsidized Stafford Loan)
USED	U.S. Department of Education

FINANCIAL AID TERMS—CLEARLY DEFINED

Accrued interest: Interest that accumulates on the unpaid principal balance of your loan.

Capitalization of interest: Addition of accrued interest to the principal balance of your loan that increases both your total debt and your monthly payments.

Disbursement: Loan funds issued by the lender.

Deferment: A period when a borrower who meets certain criteria may suspend loan payments.

Default: Failure to repay your educational loan.

Delinquency: Failure to make payments when due.

Forbearance: Temporary adjustment to a repayment schedule for cases of financial hardship.

Grace period: A specified period of time after you graduate or leave school during which you need not make payments.

Holder: The institution that currently owns your loan.

In-school, grace, and deferment interest subsidy: Interest the federal government pays for borrowers on some loans while the borrower is in school, during authorized deferments, and during grace periods.

Interest-only payment: A payment that covers only interest owed on the loan and none of the principal balance.

Interest: Cost you pay to borrow money.

Lender (Originator): The institution that puts up the money when you take out a loan. Most lenders are financial institutions, but some state agencies and schools make loans, too.

Origination fee: A fee, deducted from the principal, that is paid to the federal government to offset its cost of the subsidy to borrowers under certain loan programs.

Principal: The amount you borrow, which may increase as a result of capitalization of interest, and the amount on which you pay interest.

Promissory note: A contract between you and the lender that includes all the terms and conditions under which you promise to repay your loan.

Secondary markets: Institutions that buy student loans from originating lenders, thus providing lenders with funds to make new loans.

Servicer: The organization that administers and collects your loan. It may be either the holder of your loan or an agent acting on behalf of the holder.

Subsidized Stafford Loans: Loans based on financial need. The government pays the interest on a subsidized Stafford Loan for borrowers while they are in school and during specified deferment periods.

Unsubsidized Stafford Loans: Loans available to borrowers regardless of family income. Unsubsidized Stafford Loan borrowers are responsible for the interest during in-school, deferment, and repayment periods.

FINANCIAL AID RESOURCES

In addition to the sources listed throughout this chapter, the following are additional resources that may be used to obtain more information about financial aid.

Telephone Numbers

Federal Student Aid Information Center
(U.S. Department of Education)

Hotline	800-4-FED-AID, 800-433-3243
TDD number for the hearing-impaired	800-730-8913
For suspicion of fraud or abuse of federal aid	800-MIS-USED (800-647-8733)
Selective Service	847-688-6888
Immigration and Naturalization (INS)	415-705-4205
Internal Revenue Service (IRS)	800-829-1040
Social Security Administration	800-772-1213
National Merit Scholarship Corporation	708-866-5100
Sallie Mae's College AnswerSM Service	800-222-7183
Career College Association	202-336-6828
American College Test (ACT) (about forms submitted to the need analysis servicer)	916-361-0656
College Scholarship Service (CSS)	609-771-7725
TDD	609-883-7051

Need Access/Need Analysis Service   800-282-1550

FAFSA on the Web processing/software problems   800-801-0576

Websites

www.ed.gov/prog_info/SFAStudentGuide

The Student Guide is a free informative brochure about financial aid and is available on-line at the Department of Education's Website listed here.

www.ed.gov\prog_info\SFA\FAFSA

This site offers students help in completing the FAFSA.

www.ed.gov/offices/OPE/t4_codes.html

This website offers a list of Title IV school codes that you may need to complete the FAFSA.

www.ed.gov/offices/OPE/express.html

This website enables you to fill out and submit the FAFSA on-line. You'll need to print out, sign, and send in the release and signature pages.

www.career.org

This is the website of the Career College Association (CCA), which offers a limited number of scholarships for attendance at private proprietary schools. You can also contact the CCA at 750 First Street NE, Suite 900, Washington, DC 20002-4242.

www.salliemae.com

This website for Sallie Mae contains information about loan programs.

Software Programs

Cash for Class
Tel: 800-205-9581
FAX: 714-673-9039

Redheads Software, Inc.
  3334 East Coast Highway #216
  Corona del Mar, CA 92625
  E-mail: cashclass@aol.com

C-LECT Financial Aid Module
  800-622-7284, 315-497-0330
  Fax: 315-497-3359

Chronicle Guidance Publications
  PO Box 1190
  Moravia, NY 13118-1190

Peterson's Award Search
  PO Box 2123
  Princeton, NJ 08543-2123
  800-338-3282, 609-243-9111
  E-mail: custsvc@petersons.com

Pinnacle Peak Solutions (Scholarships 101)
  7735 East Windrose Drive
  Scottsdale, AZ 85260
  800-762-7101, 602-951-9377
  Fax: 602-948-7603

TP Software—Student Financial Aid Search Software
  PO Box 532
  Bonita, CA 91908-0532
  800-791-7791, 619-496-8673
  E-mail: mail@tpsoftware.com

Books and Pamphlets

Cassidy, Daniel J. *The Scholarship Book 2000: The Complete Guide to Private-Sector Scholarships, Fellowships, Grants, and Loans for the Undergraduate* (Englewood Cliffs, NJ: Prentice Hall, 1999).

Chany, Kalman A., and Geoff Martz. *Student Advantage Guide to Paying for College*, 1997 ed. (New York: Random House, The Princeton Review, 1997).

College School Service. *College Costs & Financial Aid Handbook*, 18th ed. (New York: The College Entrance Examination Board, 1998).

Cook, Melissa L. *College Student's Handbook to Financial Assistance and Planning* (Traverse City, MI: Moonbeam Publications, Inc., 1991).

Davis, Kristen. *Financing College: How to Use Savings, Financial Aid, Scholarships, and Loans to Afford the School of Your Choice* (Washington, DC: Random House, 1996).

Hern, Davis, and Joyce Lain Kennedy. *College Financial Aid for Dummies* (New York: IDG Books Worldwide, 1999).

How Can I Receive Financial Aid for College? Parent Brochures, ACCESS ERIC , www.ericae.net. Order a printed copy by calling 800-LET-ERIC, or write to ACCESS ERIC, Research Boulevard—MS 5F, Rockville, MD 20850-3172.

Peterson's Guides, *Peterson's Scholarships, Grants and Prizes: Guide to College Financial Aid from Private Sources* (Princeton, NJ: Peterson's, 1998).

Ragins, Marianne. *Winning Scholarships for College: An Insider's Guide* (New York: Henry Holt & Co., 1994).

Schlacter, Gail, and R. David Weber. *Scholarships 2000* (New York: Kaplan, 1999).

Schwartz, John. *College Scholarships and Financial Aid* (New York: Macmillan, Simon & Schuster, 1995).

U.S. Department of Education. *Looking for Student Aid.* This is an overview of sources of information about financial aid. To get a printed copy, call 800-4-FED-AID.

U.S. Department of Education. *The Student Guide.* This is the Department's handbook about federal aid programs. To get a printed copy, call 800-4-FED-AID.

Other Related Financial Aid Books

Annual Register of Grant Support (Chicago: Marquis, annual).

A's and B's of Academic Scholarships (Alexandria, VA: Octameron, annual).

Chronicle Student Aid Annual (Moravia, NY: Chronicle Guidance, annual).

College Blue Book: Scholarships, Fellowships, Grants and Loans (New York: Macmillan, annual).

College Financial Aid Annual (New York: Prentice-Hall, annual).

Directory of Financial Aids for Minorities (San Carlos, CA: Reference Service Press, biennial).

Directory of Financial Aids for Women (San Carlos, CA: Reference Service Press, biennial).

Financial Aids for Higher Education (Dubuque: Wm. C. Brown, biennial).

Financial Aid for the Disabled and their Families (San Carlos, CA: Reference Service Press, biennial).

Leider, Ann, and Robert Leider. *Don't Miss Out: The Ambitious Student's Guide to Financial Aid* (Alexandria, VA: Octameron, annual).

Paying Less for College (Princeton, NJ: Peterson's Guides, annual).

INSIDE TRACK

Captain Timothy Whitaker EMT-P AAS

Training Officer & Shift Supervisor

Sandusky County EMS

Fremont, Ohio

I started as an EMT-Basic after leaving the military in 1984, when I was 38 years old, although I have been interested in EMS since I was a kid. I have always been a full-time EMT with our system, but I also have a lot of other experience, such as working in large hospital emergency rooms, ground MICU transport, and worldwide fixed-wing air-ambulance transport. I am currently also an EMS educator and have lectured across the state.

I love helping other people and seeing positive outcomes from our care. The feeling of being the public's emergency care provider gives me a lot of satisfaction, even though I think that we deserve more respect and appreciation. Also, being a father, I have a special mission of my own to educate as many parents and children as I can on as many safety issues as I can.

My typical shift is a 24–48, which I love. Since we serve an entire county, including a small urban area, we are fairly busy—we have 3,500 runs a year, and this is increasing. I operate a supervisor vehicle while on duty. We cover a lot of the area's highway system and a portion of the Ohio Turnpike. Trauma is common in the summer months, but we usually have a nice mix of calls. There are some days when we take a beating, but it is mostly a nice steady shift. Occasionally we even get to sleep all night.

My administrative duties include departmental training and maintaining certification records. I also manage the entire system's operations during my shift. This means spot inspections, paperwork transfer, supply requests, et cetera. I also first respond on all critical or multipatient calls and handle all DOA [dead on arrival] calls.

There has been constant change since I entered EMS. I never thought I'd have such a broad spectrum of medications and treatments to use—today we even employ sedation in the field and a 12-lead EKG. There's always a new piece of equipment to use. A lot of the basics have remained the same, but the advanced care has just taken off.

I would advise anyone considering a career in EMS to expect to get from this career what you put into it. Love your fellow man no matter what, or you will not be able to be successful. Also, definitely earn a degree in EMS. I think the field is leaning toward degrees rather than licensure and certification.

CHAPTER four

FINDING AND APPLYING FOR A JOB

FINDING A job opening and then competing for that job can be tough. How can you discover who's hiring, get through the application process successfully, and end up with a job offer? This chapter tells you what you need to know. You'll find statistics and information on the employment outlook for EMTs in various positions. Also included is information about the query letter, resume, and interview process, as well as the various methods of finding a job, such as searching help wanted ads, using the Internet, and networking. Detailed information on the certification and application process for a range of EMT positions is covered, and sample applications are included, along with insider tips from a variety of current EMTs.

THE BEST source for employment leads for recent graduates of the EMT-Basic program is the school or agency that provided the training. EMTs can also apply directly to local ambulance services, hospitals, fire and police departments, county and city offices, and private and public employment agencies. However, because new graduates may face stiff competition if they are seeking full-time paid positions, volunteering is always a positive option for finding an appropriate opening or gaining experience in order to prepare for certification. Volunteers are always needed, and you can apply to all the above-named agencies or directly to the first aid squad in your community to become a volunteer.

As Dwaine Massey, a fire officer–EMT-Intermediate from Athens, Georgia, explains:

I really didn't think about becoming a firefighter until a friend mentioned it. It sounded interesting, so I volunteered at the local county station for a while to find out if I liked it. When an opening came up, I took the appropriate application measures and became a firefighter. I wasn't sure about being an EMT. I had never thought about that either, but it became another facet of the job of fire fighting because fire stations require that an EMT be on duty. We are around accident victims that require immediate attention, and sometimes we are the first on the scene. I applied with the county, and when an EMT opening came up, I got in for training. The county paid for the courses and equipment, which was a great opportunity. I really enjoy my job, and knowing that I can help people even more makes a big difference. I'm still a firefighter, but now I am certified to give further aid when needed. If I had never volunteered, I wouldn't be where I am today.

CONDUCTING YOUR JOB SEARCH

You've taken a training program and passed the exam; now it is time to use your skills by finding a job as an EMT. There are many ways to locate a position, and the more of them you use, the greater your chances of finding a number of openings. If you are willing to consider moving to an area of the country with greater job prospects, you can increase your chances even more. Remember that most people apply for many jobs before they are finally accepted.

Staying organized during your job search will help the entire process run smoothly. You'll want to remember when you sent out resumes, when you first contacted each prospective employer, and when you should follow up with a phone call after an interview. Keeping a calendar on which you record all of your job search activities will make it much less likely that you'll forget any important details.

Help Wanted Ads

Reading the classified ads of your local newspapers, trade journals, and professional magazines is one way to find a job as an EMT. When scanning the ads, look for the following job titles: emergency medical technician, EMT, emergency medical service, EMS, ambulance technician, rescue squad, health care, EMT-A, EMT-B, EMT-I, EMT-P, and paramedic. When you find a job posting that interests you, follow the instructions contained in it. You may be asked to phone, send a resume, or fill out an application. Record the date of your initial contact, and make a note to phone the employer within two or three weeks if you haven't heard anything.

Help wanted ads are found in many trade magazines and journals, such as *EMS Magazine* and the *Journal of Emergency Medical Services*. Not only are these good places to find advertisements, but their articles are an excellent way to keep up-to-date on current emergency medical trends as well. Both of these publications also maintain websites, listed below.

JUST THE FACTS

Flight Paramedics

There are more than 275 agencies and organizations around the country that conduct air rescue operations, with approximately 1,200 flight paramedics serving in this capacity. These positions are in high demand—for each opening, about 250 people apply.

Online Resources

The Internet has become a great place to scout for jobs. There are many general career centers online that contain classified ads. They are easily searchable using any of the job titles you might look for in classified ads found in newspapers and magazines. For example, at www.career.mosaic.com and www.jobweb.org, there are job listings for EMTs.

There are also field-specific websites aimed at those already in or looking to get into the health field. EMS magazines and journals online and the websites of newsgroups that advertise jobs, such as www.jems.com, website of the *Journal of Emergency Medical Services*, and www.medsearch.com, are good sources. Some hospitals and companies also have websites that list job openings, such as www.medctr.ucla.edu (UCLA Medical Center's website) and www.reidhosp.com (the website of Reid Hospital and Health Care Services, in Richmond, Indiana).

To find more websites, use a search engine such as Yahoo.com. Enter terms such as "hospitals," "fire departments," and "ambulance centers," or search for the name of a particular hospital or ambulance center to see if it has a website listed and classified ads. See the table below for more job-related addresses.

General Career Websites

These sites not only contain job listings, but also offer help with every aspect of job hunting, from the writing of resumes and cover letters to improving interview skills.

www.careercity.com

www.careerpath.com

www.careershop.com/healthleaders

www.cweb.com

www.hotjobs.com

www.jobs.com

www.medbulletin.com/scripts/medscape/browse.pl/param00001

www.medsearch.com

www.monster.com

www.myjobsearch.com

Specific Websites for EMT Jobs

www.emsjobs.com

www.emsvillage.comresource_center/jobs/

www.hotnursejobs.com

www.jems.com/careerpath/careerpath.html

www.jobscience.com

www.medhunters.com

www.medsearch.com

www.paramedicjobs.com

Networking Your Way into a Job

Networking may be the best way to find prospective EMT career opportunities. As Dwaine Massey mentioned at the beginning of this chapter, it can open doors you never thought existed. The people holding the doorknobs are your friends or acquaintances already working in the field. A reference from one of them can give you an advantage over job candidates who don't have or aren't using a network. Prospective employers will usually hire the candidate recommended by an employee; the more highly regarded the employee, the more his or her recommendation will count.

What Is Networking?

Networking means calling and talking with friends, acquaintances, and others who may know about EMT jobs, for advice and support. This method of job searching is also referred to as word of mouth, because it involves communication from person to person, rather than from person to job advertisement to person. If you would like to work as a firefighter-EMT, get in touch with all the people you know who work in fire departments or who have friends or relatives in the field. The more people who know about your job search and qualifications, the greater your chances of finding a job through networking.

Through networking, you may discover an opening in the hidden job market, a term referring to those jobs that are never advertised, which account for 70–80% of all job vacancies. This market exists because of the large number of employers who find employees through word of mouth. Coming to a prospective employer on the recommendation of a contact will give you a competitive edge over other candidates. A 1989 study by the American Association of Counseling and Development (AACD) showed that

▶ more than 50% of all jobs were found through networking (probably a conservative figure)
▶ those jobs were frequently higher paying, higher status jobs
▶ 25% of those who got jobs through networking stayed in the job longer
▶ better jobs were obtained through acquaintances than through friends

In today's competitive climate, successful candidates are the ones who use networking in their search for a position. Steve Patts, an EMT-Basic from Phoenix, Arizona, explains how networking even helped him enter a training program:

> To get into the EMT program at the closest school, I had to have a referral from a working EMT. I didn't know anyone who was an EMT, but my wife did. She has an uncle who works as a paramedic at a hospital ambulance service. She asked him if he could help me. He told me to come ride third on his ambulance team, where I would just watch and not help. I did, and he wrote me a referral just like that. I was in the program as soon as the next one started.

Begin networking by making a list of everyone you know in the EMS field. Depending on your relationship with each person, send a note or make a phone call to everyone on the list. You might even include your resume or call and ask people if they'd mind if you sent them a copy. Think about how you can begin making yourself more attractive to employers. Use your informal interviewing skills when you network with others.

Next, consider every other possible living, breathing, human resource. Areas to draw from include your family, friends, neighbors, school (teachers, counselors, and administrators), previous employment (employers, coworkers, and competitors), professionals (practicing EMTs), and community (business people, clubs, associations, the chamber of commerce, and religious groups). You can also use magazine articles, newspapers, or other general publicity to begin targeting people you would like to include in your network.

It is important not to overlook any possibilities. However, you shouldn't use a contact's name without receiving prior permission. Those in your network could be contacted by a prospective employer, so they should be made aware of your search and asked if they will recommend you. Once you have received the networking information, it is then up to you to get the job.

Organizing Your Contact List

As with your job search in general, networking will work better if you are organized. You may use the calendar you began for your search, a Rolodex, or even a simple notepad. The important thing is to keep track of your contacts. Index cards, a spiral notebook, a personal organizer, or a computerized database will also work. Set up your network file to include the following contact information:

- ▶ name of contact
- ▶ address and telephone number
- ▶ how you met this person
- ▶ occupation
- ▶ date last contacted
- ▶ conversation summary
- ▶ names of referrals
- ▶ date of thank-you letter
- ▶ other comments

Making Contact

The key to networking success lies in understanding that you aren't asking for a giant favor that creates a debt and gives others leverage over you. Instead, you are subtly empowering the other party while not asking for much in return. In other words, the people in your network have information or contacts that could help you find a job. When networking, you are asking people for that information.

Remember that your contacts' willingness to help you will depend largely on how your requests are formed. Keep your requests for help brief, conversational, and low-key. Be sincere. When you call:

- ▶ Recite what you plan to say before you actually make that important call.
- ▶ Ask contacts if they have time to talk for about 10 minutes, then ask for their help in sharing with you any information they may have about job openings.
- ▶ Say you don't expect an immediate answer, and ask if you could call them back or meet them at a specific date and time.
- ▶ Use phrases such as "if I could make an appointment to talk" or "if we could meet for a few minutes so that I might get your thoughts and opinions about some job search ideas I've been thinking about" or "if

I could drop in on you at work for a few minutes and pick your brain"
or "if I could get some advice on getting some exposure in the emergency medical services market."

▶ Keep it light and pleasant.

▶ Thank those you called for their time, and those you wrote for their
attention to your letter; tell them how much you appreciate their help,
and that you are grateful for their willingness to mention you to their
colleagues.

▶ Let them know that you will keep them posted on where things go
from here; most contacts will be interested to know that their input
actually helped you.

Expanding Your Contacts

Ask the people you contact for other contacts, known as referrals. Your contacts may want to call the referrals first, to find out if they mind becoming
a contact for you. Referrals will probably be strangers to you, but they
should be contacted like others in your network. Remember that you are
paying them a compliment by contacting them. People like to talk about
themselves, and everyone likes a good listener when they're giving their personal advice, information, and wisdom.

Maintaining Your Contacts

The key to faster success in your networking efforts is follow-up. The
majority of follow-up calls aren't going to produce valuable new information
or insights, but they'll succeed in reminding people of who you are. You will
be gratified to see how often one of these calls proves timely and serves to
jog a contact's short-term memory. You should also write a thank-you note
to everyone you speak to formally about your job search. The notes will help
to keep your name and job search visible.

CONSIDERING RELOCATION

Taking into account the possibility that the area in which you live may not
provide many salaried positions, consider being flexible about location. A
willingness to relocate could help new EMTs gain a foothold on the career

ladder. In some small rural areas, salaried positions are hard to find because of a strong tradition of volunteer ambulance services. In larger and more populated areas, the demand for EMTs is much greater, so if a technician is willing to relocate to an area where the demand is higher, such as a large city like Chicago or Los Angeles, he or she would have a better chance of finding employment.

There are also many international paramedic employers, who provide a host of job opportunities to those who seek travel and adventure in addition to employment. Many of these positions involve the oil industry; paramedics are needed to provide medical services to oil workers in remote locations such as offshore and desert drilling sites. There are also opportunities in foreign hospitals, mining operations, remote research stations, fishing industry sites, and remote or foreign ambulance services. Check Appendix A for a listing of international paramedic employers, complete with contact information.

IN THE NEWS

EMS and Bioterrorism

The U.S. Department of Health and Human Services is spending $278 million during fiscal year 2001 to prepare for the growing threat of bioterrorism. This is an area of increased training and emphasis in EMS, as EMS personnel are an integral part of the response to any such incident.

WRITING AN INQUIRY LETTER

Once you've found a job opening, your next step is to contact the hiring company. This initial contact is usually on paper, in the form of a cover letter. As with any other type of contact with a potential employer, you need to make a good impression. The letter you send should be typed neatly and proofread for any spelling or grammar errors. A good cover letter should also be clear, direct, and no longer than three or four paragraphs. You should send your letter to a specific person, either the personnel director or the department head for whom you would be directly working. If you don't know the person's name, call the EMS center and ask to whom you should write.

Begin your letter by explaining why you are writing. Let the person know that you are inquiring about possible job openings at the company, that you are responding to an advertisement in a particular publication, or that someone recommended that you write. Introduce the information on your resume, which you should include. Add information that shows you are suited for the job at the EMT level for which you are applying. End by thanking the reader for his or her attention to your letter, and add that you look forward to hearing from him or her soon. The following pages contain some examples that may be used for reference when creating your own personalized cover letter.

180 Meadow Court

City, State 12345

November 10, 2000

Mr. John Haroldson

St. Mary's Ambulance Center

PO Box 4545

City, State 12345

Dear Mr. Haroldson:

I am writing to inquire about your need for Emergency Medical Technicians at your ambulance center. I have heard many favorable things about your ambulance services, and I feel that this would be the perfect work environment for me. I am very interested in an available position.

I recently graduated from the EMT-Basic program at Med Tech Community College and have received the required state and national certification. I received hands-on experience and training in the Med Tech School's training ambulance center, and I believe I am in top physical condition, ready to begin work as an EMT-B.

I have always been interested in helping people in emergency situations, and this interest increased after living through such a situation myself. When I entered the EMT-Basic program, I realized my potential in becoming a great worker under pressure, as well as a caring individual for those under duress.

I have enclosed my resume and am available to meet with you at your convenience. I can also arrange for you to speak with my references. I can be reached at 343-555-7676 or at the address above. Thank you for your attention. I look forward to hearing from you.

Sincerely,

Mary Van Doren

543 Stratford Drive
Anytown, State 12345

April 7, 2001

Ms. Joan Embers
Chark County Ambulance Service
PO Box 4456
City, State 12346

Dear Ms. Embers:

I am writing in response to your advertisement in the Sunday, March 23, 2001, *Maryland Journal and Constitution.* I have researched your emergency ambulance service and have found many attractive aspects that make your company an excellent work environment.

The advertisement stated that you are looking for someone with experience as an EMT-Intermediate. I am a recent graduate of North Maryland Technology's EMT-Intermediate program, and I have the appropriate certification. I am looking for just this type of employment.

I have a good rapport with patients, doctors, and other EMTs and work well without constant supervision. Most important, I am completely dedicated to my work. I pride myself on making sure every victim rescued is treated with compassion and skill.

If you wish to hire an EMT-Intermediate who is good under pressure, experienced, and completely dedicated, I believe I am your candidate. I have the talent, the knowledge, and the training to be a successful EMT.

Enclosed is my resume. I am available to meet with you at your convenience and can be reached at 242-555-8786 or at the address above. Thank you for your attention to my letter. I look forward to hearing from you.

Sincerely,
Mike Anderson

WRITING YOUR RESUME

The word *resume* originates from the French word *résumer*, meaning "to summarize." Your resume will be a brief outline of your education, work experience, and special abilities and skills. This summary can act as your introduction by mail or as your calling card if you are applying in person. Although a resume may not be required for getting an EMT position, it's worth it to put one together in case an employer asks for it. Your resume can also be used as a reference for you when you are filling out application forms or preparing to be interviewed.

A resume is meant to capture the interest of potential employers, so they will call you for a personal interview. That means you want to highlight your:

► career objective(s)
► education
► employment history and related experience
► special skills and/or personal qualifications

Select only those facts that point out your relevant skills and experiences. At the top of your resume, write your name, address, phone number, and e-mail address. Then decide which items will be most interesting to the employer you plan to contact. Be sure to provide accurate, truthful information. Expect that anything on your resume may be scrutinized during a background check later in the selection process.

Objective

Under your name and address, you will need to state your job objective, which is your reason for contacting the employer. After the heading Objective, describe briefly what you hope to accomplish in your job search, such as becoming an EMT-Basic.

Educational Background

List the schools you have attended in reverse chronological order, starting with your most recent training and ending with the least recent. Employers want to know at a glance what your highest qualifications are. For each educational experience, include dates attended, name and location of school, and degree or certificate earned. If you have not attended college, end with your high school; if you have attended college, it is not necessary to list your high school.

Work Experience

List your relevant work experience, including volunteering. If you don't have any relevant experience yet, connect any employment experiences you've had to the skills and traits of a successful EMT. Your potential employer is looking for someone who can work well under pressure and deal effectively with the public, as well as being in good physical condition. Find ways to connect summer jobs, volunteer experiences, and/or part-time employment with the development of these skills and traits. Keep these job descriptions brief.

Special Skills

You may wish to include another section called "Special Skills," "Skills," or "Personal Qualifications." Write down any skills, such as knowledge of medical language, knowledge of ambulance equipment, physical abilities, and any other related expertise you posses, that you think might help you land an EMT job.

Ways to Organize Your Resume

There are different ways to organize the information on your resume. Depending on your education and work experiences, you may want to emphasize one while de-emphasizing the other. Read through the descriptions of the various resume styles to decide which will work best for you.

▶ The Chronological Resume

The most common resume format summarizes your work experience year by year. Begin with your current or most recent employment and then work backward. For each job, list the name and location of the company for which you worked, the dates you were employed, and the position(s) you held. The order in which you present this information will depend on what you are trying to emphasize. For instance, if you want to call attention to the type or level of job you held, you should put the job title first. Then use this order consistently for each work experience listed. Summer employment or part-time work should be labeled as such, and you will need to specify the months in the dates of employment for positions held less than a year.

▶ The Functional Resume

This type of resume emphasizes what you can do rather than what you have done. It is useful for people who have large gaps in their work history or who have relevant skills that would not be properly highlighted in a chronological listing of jobs. The functional resume concentrates on your qualifications, which may be anything from familiarity with hospital procedures to organizational skills or managerial experience. Specific jobs may be mentioned, but they are not the primary focus. This type of resume would be good for the person with little work experience.

▶ The Combination Resume

You may decide that a combination of the chronological and the functional resume would best highlight your skills. A combination resume allows for a mixture of your skills with a chronological list of jobs you've held. You get the best of both resumes. This is an excellent choice for students who have limited work experience and who want to highlight specific skills.

Be sure to check out the general employment websites listed on page 96. Many of them contain excellent information on resume writing, samples, and even online help.

Sample Chronological Resume

JANICE LITTLE

1234 Murray Hill Drive

Dallas, TX 12345

214-555-2143

E-mail: jlittle@server.com

OBJECTIVE	To obtain an EMT-Basic position
EDUCATION	EMT-Basic certificate, June 1997
	Med Tech Institute
	20 Troost Avenue, Dallas, TX 12345
	GPA 3.95
	Armadillo High School, Dallas, TX 12345
	June, 1996
	GPA 3.98
WORK EXPERIENCE	Candy Striper, nurse aide volunteer, 1995-1996
	St. Mary's Hospital, Dallas, TX 12345
	• Served meals and helped patients eat, dress, and bathe
	• Delivered messages and answered patient call bells
	• Completed daily filing and answered telephones
	• Inventoried, stored, and moved supplies
	Assistant Evening Manager, 1994–1995
	Texan Steer Restaurant, Dallas, TX 12345
	• Began waiting on tables and greeting customers
	• Took over arranging staff schedule
	• Balanced register and deposited money
	• Learned how to order food and soft drinks
	• Managed personnel when manager was absent
HONORS AND AWARDS	Student of the Year, Med Tech Institute, Dallas, TX.
ACTIVITIES	Volunteering at Oak View Nursing Home in Dallas, TX
	Swimming, running, kayaking
	Volunteering at local food shelters
REFERENCES	References furnished upon request

Sample Functional Resume

MIKE ANDERSON

1234 Darcey Avenue

Trellis, MD 12346

301-555-1244

OBJECTIVE	To obtain a position as an EMT-Intermediate
VOLUNTEER EMT	Two years' volunteer experience as an EMT-Basic in volunteer fire station part-time • Performed typical EMT-Basic duties • Monitored patient status • Kept ambulance in working condition
EMT-BASIC	EMT-Basic for two years at private ambulance service • Performed typical EMT-Basic duties • Monitored patient status • Kept ambulance in working condition
EDUCATION	EMT-Intermediate certificate, March 1998 University of Maryland Medical Center, Trellis, MD GPA 3.8–4.0 EMT-Basic certificate, January 1996 Medical Institute of Maryland, Trellis, MD GPA: 3.9–4.0
REFERENCES	References furnished upon request

Sample Combination Resume

CATHY WALTERS

1234 Glenwood Street

Glenwood, CO 12347

303-555-4321

OBJECTIVE	To gain a career position as an EMT-Paramedic

QUALIFICATIONS

Skilled EMT-Paramedic

- Good rapport with patients
- Expertise in all areas of Emergency Medical Services
- Knowledgeable in life saving procedures
- Devoted to patient care

EDUCATION

EMT-Paramedic certification, June 2000

Colorado Mountain College, Glenwood Springs, CO

GPA 3.8–4.0

EMT-Intermediate certification, June 1997

Colorado Mountain College, Glenwood Springs, CO

GPA 4.0

EMT-Basic certification, June 1994

Colorado Mountain College, Glenwood Springs, CO

GPA: 3.8–4.0

CLINICAL TRAINING

Paramedic training includes

- Administering IV Therapy
- Advanced cardiac support
- Use of adjunctive equipment
- Drug administration

EMT-I and EMT-B training includes

- CPR certification
- Patient care
- Cardiology
- Pharmacology
- Megacodes
- Advanced airway management
- Ambulance upkeep

RELATED EXPERIENCE

EMT-Basic, St. Francis Ambulance Center, Glenwood

Springs, CO

1/1995–12/1997

- Performed typical EMT-Basic duties
- Monitored patient status
- Kept ambulance in working condition

EMT-Intermediate, Glenwood Springs County Fire Department

2/1998–12/1999

- Performed typical EMT-Intermediate duties
- Drove ambulance on occasion
- Performed advanced patient procedures
- Monitored patient status

REFERENCES

References available upon request

Resume Writing Tips

- Be neat and organized.
- Increase your resume's legibility by effectively using white space.
- Try to limit your resume to one page, but do not crowd; use two pages if necessary.
- Use action verbs.
- Be consistent in style.
- Be positive and confident, but don't lie or embellish.
- Use a conservative font, and use white, cream, or gray paper.
- Investigate employment sites on the Internet for sample resumes and online help.

THE SELECTION PROCESS

Earlier in this chapter you learned about the many ways in which to find job openings. Once you've found one, your next step will be to contact the hiring company. Among most hospitals, private ambulance companies, and state- or county-run EMS facilities, the hiring procedures are similar. They begin with an application. If everything on your application looks good, you will be asked to undergo a medical exam and drug testing, to ensure that you are drug free and healthy and don't have any physical limitations that could prevent you from performing your job duties.

Many employers also conduct criminal background checks, looking closely at all the information you provided on your application, as inspecting your driving record and screening your references. At some point during the hiring process, you will be asked to perform an ambulance road test. Finally, if every other step of the process has gone well, you will be asked to sit for an interview.

If you are planning to become a firefighter or a police officer, you will have additional steps included in the selection process. To work in either profession you must undergo a written test, a physical agility test, training in a police or fire academy, and a psychological evaluation.

The EMS facility to which you're applying may give you a job description showing the nature of the duties and experience required for the position. Although job titles may differ among various institutions, the positions are basically the same. Below is an example of a job posting for an EMT-

Basic from a hospital ambulance service. Note that this position is also referred to as EMT-A (for ambulance) and EMT-I (for level 1).

EMT-Basic, EMT-A, EMT-I

Job Summary	Provides direct patient emergency care according to emergency policy and procedure. Contributes to the safe and effective operation of the ambulance unit. Provides life saving techniques for emergency patients.
Education	High school, EMT-Basic certification
Licensure	None
Experience	Previous exposure to training
Skills	Skills basic to completion of EMT-Basic course
Essential Physical and Mental Functions and Environmental Conditions	Able to communicate medically using medical terminology

Able to assess injury severity and perform CPR and other required basic lifesaving techniques

Able to communicate calmly and rationally under consistent pressure

Able to see objects far away

Able to discriminate color and perceive depth

Able to give and receive verbal communications

Able to read and write written communications, such as reports.

Able to carry objects 10 pounds or heavier frequently, 49 pounds or less rarely.

Able to perform motor skills such as bending, twisting, turning, kneeling, reaching out, reaching up, wrist turning, grasping, finger manipulation, feeling perception, and fast response frequently

Information Interview

Before you begin formally interviewing for job openings, it is a good idea to perform an information interview with an EMT professional you know who is already in the type of position you want. This will arm you with some knowledge of your interviewer's occupation and your own interests, abilities, and values, so you will be better prepared on your job interview. Ask pertinent questions, get full information, take a tour of the facility, and you will be a step ahead of the competition. Here is a list of questions that will help you get the information you want in an information interview:

▶ How would you describe your work, in general?

▶ What is your typical workday like?

▶ What things do you find most rewarding about your work?

▶ What are the toughest problems or frustrations that you encounter in your job?

▶ What compromises are the most difficult to make?

▶ If you could change your job in some way, what would that change be?

▶ What are the trade/professional/union groups to which you belong, and which do you find most beneficial in your work? Do any of them assist students who are interested in entry-level positions in your field?

▶ What abilities, interests, values, and personality characteristics are important for effectiveness and satisfaction in your field?

▶ How do people usually learn about job openings in your field?

▶ If you were hiring someone for an entry-level position in your field, what would be the critical factors influencing your choice of one candidate over another?

▶ Is there anything else you think I would benefit from knowing about this field?

By conducting an information interview, not only will you be more knowledgeable about your prospective position, but you will also gain interview experience, which may lessen the anxiety in your job interview.

The Application

Once you've found a job opening and inquired about the position, you'll learn how the hiring company gathers applications. You may be sent an application in the mail, or may be asked to come to the company's location to fill it out. Some companies have applications on their websites that you can fill out online and e-mail back.

Many employers still prefer that you fill out their application on site; if this is the case with your prospective employer, bring all the information you may need to fill out the form correctly and completely. You should also bring along several copies of your resume and turn in one with your application. Many times an EMT supervisor, employment recruiter, or personnel department head will talk briefly with you at the time you turn in your application. Make your first impression a good one by being prepared and neatly dressed.

If you have ever filled out an application for any kind of job, school, or financial aid before, the application for an EMT position will be familiar. Expect to be asked for the following:

▶ name, address, and social security number
▶ job information or previous work experience, including dates, reason for leaving, and salary
▶ skills or supervisory experience
▶ educational experience
▶ criminal background information
▶ references
▶ citizenship status

Because of the federal law prohibiting discrimination, no question on the application form should touch upon a prospective employee's race, color, religion, national origin, sex, marital status, or disability. If there is a question on the application referring to any of these topics, you have the option of leaving it blank. You will, however be asked to give your age. Since most EMTs have to drive an ambulance at one time or another, they need to be covered by their company's automobile insurance policy.

Insurance regulations specify the age at which someone can begin coverage, which is usually 21 or 25.

You will be asked to sign the application to verify that all the information is true and correct. At the bottom, there may be a statement of understanding and a reference release stating that any incorrect information is cause for immediate dismissal. Therefore, it is imperative that you give only correct, truthful information. Expect that later in the hiring process, everything you have written will be checked during a background investigation. Those who falsify information on their application are out of the process. As an EMT supervisor at University Hospital in Jacksonville, Florida, says:

> We have interviewed applicants that seem perfect for the position. Their answers to the questions we ask couldn't be more perfect, and their references look wonderful. That is until we check the references. One time it turned out that when we called a job reference, he told us not to hire the person. And, when we called the school listed, a representative said the person had never attended. My advice is never to falsify any information on your resume or application. Honesty is very important in your job as an EMT. We need to be able to trust you with people's lives. We were very disappointed but probably not as disappointed as the person who wasn't honest on the application.

Your application will stay active on file at a hospital for six months. If you have not called to update it, it will be kept inactive for another six months and then discarded. However, you may reapply or update your application at any time for other openings. In smaller EMS facilities your application may also remain on file, depending on the size of the company. However, smaller companies usually do not have as high a turnover rate as hospitals, leaving little or no need to keep applications on file.

ON THE JOB

The Mankoski Pain Scale

Andrea Mankoski devised this pain scale to help describe the subjective experience of pain in more concrete terms to her doctors and family. It is used by many in the pre-hospital care community to help determine the level of pain experienced by a patient.

0—Pain Free

1—Very minor annoyance—occasional minor twinges. No medication needed.

2—Minor annoyance—occasional strong twinges. No medication needed.

3—Annoying enough to be distracting. Mild painkillers take care of it. (Aspirin, Ibuprofen.)

4—Can be ignored if you are really involved in your work, but still distracting. Mild painkillers remove pain for 3 to 4 hours.

5—Can't be ignored for more than 30 minutes. Mild painkillers ameliorate pain for 3-4 hours.

6—Can't be ignored for any length of time, but you can still go to work and participate in social activities. Stronger painkillers (codeine, narcotics) reduce pain for 3–4 hours.

7—Makes it difficult to concentrate, interferes with sleep. You can still function with effort. Stronger painkillers are only partially effective.

8—Physical activity severely limited. You can read and converse with effort. Nausea and dizziness set in as factors of pain.

9—Unable to speak. Crying out or moaning uncontrollably—near delirium.

10—Unconscious. Pain makes you pass out.

Sample Applications

On the following pages are copies of actual applications used by real hiring companies. These applications are provided as samples only. Read through them to find out the information you'll be asked to provide and to practice filling out an application. Don't underestimate this step. Filling out the application neatly, accurately, and completely can make or break your quest for employment; it is the first step of the hiring process, and it gives your prospective employer his or her first impression of you.

City of Sacramento
Employment Application
Department of Human Resources
921 10th Street, Room 101, Sacramento, CA 95814
Telephone: (916) 264-5726 / TDD: (916) 264-7388
An Equal Opportunity/Affirmative Action Employer

INSTRUCTIONS: *This application is part of the examination process. It must be __completely filled out__ and signed to be accepted for review. Late and/or incomplete applications will be rejected.*

PLEASE PRINT OR TYPE
SOCIAL SECURITY NUMBER _____ - _____ - _____

JOB/EXAMINATION TITLE: _____

NAME _____
          Last   First   Middle Initial

MAILING ADDRESS: _____
                    Street #   Street Name   Apartment #

         City   State   Zip Code

Dept. of Human Resources Use Only	
App. Accepted	☐
App. Rejected	☐
Education	☐
Experience	☐
NMQ	☐
Late	☐
Other	☐

HOME PHONE ( ) _____ OTHER PHONE ( ) _____

ALL APPLICANTS, INCLUDING CITY EMPLOYEES, MUST IMMEDIATELY NOTIFY PERSONNEL SERVICES' STAFF, ROOM 200 AT THE ABOVE ADDRESS OF ANY ADDRESS OR PHONE CHANGES.

AGE: If applying for a sworn position in law enforcement or the fire service, will you be 21 or older at the application deadline date? _____ YES _____ NO

CALIFORNIA DRIVER LICENSE: If required for position, do you have one? ☐ Yes ☐ No
Dr. License # _____ Class _____ Expires _____

VETERAN'S PREFERENCE: Are you requesting Veteran's Preference? ☐ Yes ☐ No
To qualify for Veteran's Preference, a copy of Form DD214 **must be** submitted with this application. There are several criteria you must meet before qualifying for this preference. Please ask for the <u>VETERAN'S PREFERENCE REGULATIONS</u> sheet.

Active Duty - From _____ to _____

CONVICTIONS: Conviction of a crime is not necessarily a bar to employment. Each case is considered separately based on job requirements. However, failure to list convictions, except as provided below, may result in termination from the examination process or employment.

1.   Have you ever been convicted by a court of a crime? ☐ Yes ☐ No
    Omit: a) Traffic violations (Driving Under the Influence Convictions **must** be reported).
    Omit: b) Any conviction committed prior to your 18th birthday which was finally adjudicated in Juvenile Court or under a youth offender law.
    Omit: c) Any incident sealed under Welfare and Institutions Code S781 or Penal Code S1203.45.

2.   If "YES" state WHAT conviction, WHEN, WHERE, AND DISPOSITION OF CASE. _____

CITY EMPLOYMENT:

1.   Are you currently employed by the City of Sacramento? ☐ Yes ☐ No
    If "YES", what department? _____
2.   If "NO", have you ever been employed by the City of Sacramento? ☐ Yes ☐ No
    If "YES", what department? _____
    If you were previously employed by the City of Sacramento
    under another name, please state other name(s). _____
3.   Please check the type(s) of work you will accept:
    ☐ Permanent employment   ☐ Full-time   ☐ Part-time   ☐ Temporary (12 months maximum in any one job).

EDUCATION AND TRAINING:
Complete this section if required for job. Submit verification of your education such as copies of transcripts or diplomas.
                      High School Graduate or Passed GED? ☐ Yes ☐ No

NAME AND LOCATION OF COLLEGE, UNIVERSITY, BUSINESS, CORRESPONDENCE, TRADE OR SERVICE SCHOOL(S)	MAJOR COURSE OF STUDY	Completed # of		Diploma, Certificate, or Degree Received, # Hours of Training Program, or Course(s) Required by Job Announcement
		Semester Units	Quarter Units	

Current certificates of professional competence, licenses, membership in professional associations. _____

_____

EMPLOYMENT QUESTIONNAIRE

CHECK MALE OR FEMALE. ☐ Male ☐ Female
ALSO, PLEASE CHECK ONE BOX ONLY FOR THE RACIAL/ETHNIC CATEGORY YOU MOST CLOSELY IDENTIFY WITH.
(SEE BELOW FOR THE ETHNIC DEFINITIONS.)

☐ White   *(Not Hispanic origin) All persons having origins in any of the original peoples of Europe, North Africa, or the Middle East.*
☐ Black   *(Not of Hispanic origin) All persons having origins in any of the Black racial groups of Africa.*
☐ Hispanic   *All persons of Mexican, Puerto Rican, Cuban, any other Spanish Hispanic (does not include persons of Portuguese or Brazilian origin or persons who acquire Spanish surname).*
☐ Asian or   *All persons having origins in any of the original peoples of the Far East, Southeast Asia, the Indian Subcontinent, or the Pacific Islands (excluding the Philippine*
Pacific Islander   *Islands). This area includes, for example, China, Japan, Korea, and Samoa.*
☐ American Indian   *All persons having origins in any of the original peoples of North America, and who maintain cultural identifications through tribal affiliation or community recognition.*
or Alaskan Native   *Please identify your tribal affiliation: _____*

☐ Filipino   *All persons having origins in the Philippine Islands.*

- REVERSE SIDE MUST BE COMPLETED -

JOB/EXAMINATION TITLE: _____ NAME_____

Last   First   Middle Initial

QUALIFYING EXPERIENCE: *List experience which relates to the qualifications required on the Job Announcement.*
Begin with your most recent experience. List all jobs separately. The experience you list will be used to determine if you
meet the qualifications stated on the job announcement. Applications that do not list related experience will be considered
incomplete and will be rejected. A resume will not substitute for the information required in this section. Your application
will be rejected if you write "See Resume".

NOTE: If you have additional experience and/or comments, please attached another sheet. Qualifying experience is based on 40 hours per week
(pro-rated if less than 40 hours/week).

FROM: MO. DAY YR.	TITLE:	PRESENT OR MOST RECENT EMPLOYER:
TO: MO. DAY YR.	DUTIES:	
Total time: YR. MO.		ADDRESS:
HOURS per WEEK:		
# PEOPLE SUPERVISED:		PHONE:
MONTHLY SALARY:		SUPERVISOR:
		May we contact? ☐ YES ☐ NO
FROM: MO. DAY YR.	TITLE:	FORMER EMPLOYER:
TO: MO. DAY YR.	DUTIES:	
Total Time: YR. MO.		ADDRESS:
HOURS per WEEK:		
# PEOPLE SUPERVISED:		PHONE:
MONTHLY SALARY:		SUPERVISOR:
		May we contact? ☐ YES ☐ NO
FROM: MO. DAY YR.	TITLE:	FORMER EMPLOYER:
TO: MO. DAY YR.	DUTIES:	
Total Time: YR. MO.		ADDRESS:
HOURS per WEEK:		
# PEOPLE SUPERVISED:		PHONE:
MONTHLY SALARY:		SUPERVISOR:
		May we contact? ☐ YES ☐ NO
FROM: MO. DAY YR.	TITLE:	FORMER EMPLOYER:
TO: MO. DAY YR.	DUTIES:	
Total Time: YR. MO.		ADDRESS:
HOURS per WEEK:		
# PEOPLE SUPERVISED:		PHONE:
MONTHLY SALARY:		SUPERVISOR:
		May we contact? ☐ YES ☐ NO

I CERTIFY that all statements in this application are true and complete. I agree and understand that any misstatements or omissions of material facts
herein will cause forfeiture on my part of all rights to employment with the City of Sacramento. I understand that if I do not meet the announced
requirements, I will be eliminated from the examination process, and that applications must be received by the City Department of Human Resources at
921 10th Street, Room 101, Sacramento CA 95814, by 5:00 p.m. on the final filing date specified on the Job Announcement. POSTMARKS ARE NOT
ACCEPTED. I herby authorize the city to verify the accuracy of the information I have provided on this application.

SIGNATURE: _____   DATE:_____

(Required for application to be complete)

**THIS APPLICATION AND ALL ATTACHMENTS ARE CONSIDERED PROPERTY OF THE CITY OF SACRAMENTO
DEPARTMENT OF HUMAN RESOURCES. PHOTOCOPIES WILL NOT BE FURNISHED. PLEASE ATTACH COPIES OF
YOUR ORIGINAL DOCUMENTS.**

Job/Examination Title: _____

I first learned of this job opening through (check one only):

☐ A Friend or Relative
☐ The City's Department of Human Resources Job Line or Walk In
☐ Contact with a City Department/Employee
   If Department, Specify Which _____
☐ An Organization or Group (Specify) _____
☐ An Advertisement (Specify Newspaper, Publication,
   TV or Radio Station) _____
☐ Other Means (Specify) _____

Do you have any physical or mental impairment which may limit
your ability to perform the job applied for?   ☐ YES   ☐ NO
If yes, what can be done to accommodate your limitations and,
if necessary, to provide assistance in the testing process?

_____

_____

PER 029

CITY OF HOUSTON
PERSONNEL DEPARTMENT
P.O. BOX 1562
HOUSTON, TEXAS 77251

An Equal Opportunity Employer

EMPLOYMENT
APPLICATION

Please Print In Ink Or Type

Position: _____ PN# _____ Today's Date

PERSONAL

Last Name	First	Middle	Social Security # Must be verified

No. Street	City	State	Zip	Home Phone	Business/Alternate Phone

U. S. Citizenship ☐ YES   NO ☐   If not a citizen, do you possess a work authorization?
Number and Type

If you have ever been convicted of an offense (excluding minor traffic violations) complete the following:

Charge	Place of Arrest	Date	What Disposition was Made?

Please list below any relatives, including those by marriage, employed by the City:

Name of Relative	Relationship	Department	Position

Have you ever been employed by the City of Houston? ☐ YES   NO ☐

	Position Held	Date of Separation

Under what name did you appear on payroll?

EDUCATION

Name & Location	Date Graduated		Degree	If no, highest yr or hrs compl.	Major
	YES	NO			
High School					
College or University					
Graduate School					
Trade/Business/Technical					
Armed Service School					

MILITARY

Branch of Service	Service Dates		Rank at Discharge	Are you now a member of any military or naval organization?
	From	To		☐ YES NO ☐

Do you have a valid Texas driver's license? ☐ YES   NO ☐   _____
(TEXAS DRIVER'S LICENSE NUMBER)
(Class A, P, or C)

Do Not Write In This Space

PER 029 REV. 2-93

List below beginning with your most recent, all present and past employment.
Please complete in full.

	Name & Address of Company	Position, Dates Emp. & Salary		Supv. Name & Title	Reason for Leaving
1				Name	
		From Mo/Yr	Current $	Title	
		To Mo/Yr	Final $		
2				Name	
		From Mo/Yr		Title	
		To Mo/Yr	Final $		
3				Name	
		From Mo/Yr		Title	
		To Mo/Yr	Final $		
4				Name	
		From Mo/Yr		Title	
		To Mo/Yr	Final $		
5				Name	
		From Mo/Yr		Title	
		To Mo/Yr	Final $		

EMPLOYMENT HISTORY

List below three references (other than relatives)

Name	Phone	Address	Employer

REFERENCES

MAY WE CONTACT YOUR PRESENT EMPLOYER FOR REFERENCE? _____

PLEASE READ CAREFULLY BEFORE SIGNING: I certify that all the information provided by me in connection with my application, whether on this document or not, is true and complete, and I understand that any misstatement, falsification, or omission of information shall be grounds for refusal to hire or, if hired, termination. I authorize any of the persons, organizations, and educational institutions referenced in this application to give officials of the City of Houston any and all information concerning my previous employment, education, or any other information they might have, personal or otherwise, with regard to any of the subjects covered by this application, and I release all such parties from all liability from any damages which may result from furnishing such information to the City of Houston.

I UNDERSTAND THAT ALL PERSONS OFFERED EMPLOYMENT BY THE CITY OF HOUSTON MUST SUCCESS-FULLY PASS A DRUG TEST AS A CONDITION OF EMPLOYMENT.

_____
Signature of Applicant

_____
Date

The Medical Exam and Drug Testing

The medical exam itself is nothing unusual; it will be just like any other thorough physical exam. The doctor may be on the staff of the hiring agency or someone outside of the department with his or her own private practice. Your blood pressure, temperature, weight, and height will be measured; your heart and lungs will be listened to, ears and nose checked, and limbs examined. You will also have to donate a little blood and urine to be analyzed. Because some of these tests have to be sent out to a lab, you won't know the results of the physical exam right away. You will be notified as soon as the test results are known.

Drug screening is usually conducted at the same time the medical exam is administered, but can be done earlier in the process. Use of illegal drugs, of course, will disqualify you immediately from the process. If the test comes back positive because of a prescription drug you used, the department can ask you about it, but cannot use the condition for which the drug is prescribed to reject you because of the Americans with Disabilities Act (ADA).

Criminal Background Check

Your prospective employer will want to verify the information you provided on your application as well as contact the people you supplied as references. This may be done by someone in the company or by an outside investigator. Let your references know that they will be contacted and asked for information such as how long they have know you and what kind of employee/student/friend you are. Your driving history will be examined, so be sure to give complete, honest information on your application. The average EMS company regulations require you to have no more than two speeding tickets in the last three years and absolutely no DUIs (driving under the influence). If you are already working and receive a DUI, you may be instantly terminated by the company. Driving an ambulance is part of an EMT's job description, so the employer needs to know that every EMT has a clean record and can perform this duty without legal impediments.

Driving an Ambulance

You'll be required to take an ambulance driving course before being hired as an EMT. The company may provide the training or you may be required to seek training on your own. The formal training program ensures that you can drive through various conditions, such as at high speed and on slick roads. Susan Carpenter, and EMT-B in Cary, North Carolina, describes a driving test:

> One of the senior officers takes you out in an ambulance and gives you a street name. You need to be able to get him or her there the fastest, easiest way. This is called "learning your district." They also teach you how to read road maps.

As with the other steps in the selection process, the driving test must be successfully completed before you can be hired.

The Interview

This is the most important step in the hiring process. Not only can the impression you make on a prospective employer get you the job, but it could also determine where you become stationed and on what shift. The interview also gives you more information about the hiring company. In other words, you are also in a way interviewing them. You might discover something that makes you realize this is not the company for which you want to work.

EMT interviews are conducted much like any other. There will usually be more than one supervisor or personnel department head in the room with you. After the interview, these people will discuss your qualifications and make hiring decisions together. Firefighter-EMTs and police officer-EMTs often have oral interviews or oral boards, which take place in front of a larger panel of personnel. Some companies interview prospective EMTs twice if the supervisors who conducted your first interview think you are a good candidate.

Prepare for Your Interview

Preparation will enable you to be confident, overcome interviewing inexperience, and sell yourself and your qualifications. You should bring your resume with you, even if the company already has it, and a personal inventory (a reference of possible answers to tough questions) for your own use.

The inventory, which can be nothing more than a short personal autobiography, can help you describe your strengths and give examples to support your resume. Having it handy will help you remember things when you feel on the spot and your memory may not be what it should be. Relying on it will also help you remain confident throughout the interview.

Researching the EMS company you're applying to will help you show your genuine interest in the company during the interview. The Internet, the public library, and health publications are good sources for this kind of information. By doing this type of preparation, you will be able to converse knowledgeably about the EMS, police, or fire company during the interview.

Allow sufficient time for the interview. More than likely, you will be interviewing with more than one person during the interview cycle. You will not be at your best if you are worried about another appointment. It is a mistake to rush your interviewers because you have made a previous conflicting commitment for the same day.

Arrive at the interview early to show your respect for the interviewers as well as your professionalism. Allow extra travel time if you are unfamiliar with the employer's location to accommodate any delays.

Keep yourself in a positive frame of mind. If your interview begins on a downbeat, it may be difficult to turn the atmosphere around into a positive situation later. Remember to turn any negatives into positives right away.

A hospital EMT supervisor and interviewer gives some advice about the interview procedure:

The answers to the questions you are asked are the main points we look at when interviewing. If I ask you how you liked your past job, and you reply with how you hated it, that your boss was terrible and the workers petty, then I know what kind of worker you will be. The last thing you want to do is burn bridges with anyone who could be a reference. We want to see in you the traits that make a good EMT. Those qualities would be showing you are calm, that you can learn from mistakes, that you can make decisions quickly, and that you know how to treat patients.

Answering Tough Interview Questions

Employers tend to ask potential employees two kinds of questions: directive and open-ended. Directive questions attempt to gain, clarify, or verify factual information. Application forms are a series of directive questions. In contrast, the open-ended question is an effort to draw out strengths and weaknesses. Watch out for illegal, discriminatory questions. These questions probe for information that allows the listener to draw conclusions based on stereotypes or personal assumptions about human behavior. It is illegal for an employer to make a hiring decision based on factors such as race and religion.

To deal effectively with all types of interview questions, you need to consider the employer's point of view, and remember to stay calm. No matter what kind of question is asked, an employer really has only three actual questions:

1. Can you do the work? (Do you have the skills, competence, credentials, etc.?)
2. Will you do the work? (Do you have the motivation and stamina to produce?)
3. Can you get along with others, especially with me, your supervisor? (What are your interpersonal skills and key personality traits?)

When responding to questions, ask yourself what the underlying question is. This is particularly important with open-ended and illegally discriminatory questions. Accuracy and specificity are the keys to answering directive questions. The ability to understand yourself as a "product" and express your strengths will help you answer open-ended questions more effectively.

Below are some interview questions frequently asked by employers. Think about your answers as you read through the list.

- ▶ Why should we hire you?
- ▶ What are your career objectives?
- ▶ Tell me a little about yourself.
- ▶ If you could have the perfect position, what would it be?
- ▶ Do you have plans for continuing education?
- ▶ Why did you choose this career field?
- ▶ In what type of position are you most interested?
- ▶ What do you expect to be doing in five years?
- ▶ What is your previous work experience? What have you gained or learned from it?
- ▶ Why are you interested in our EMS company and in this particular opening?
- ▶ What do you consider to be your major strengths and weaknesses?
- ▶ In what ways do you think you can make a contribution to our service?
- ▶ What two or three accomplishments have given you the most satisfaction?
- ▶ What have you done to show initiative and willingness to work?
- ▶ What journals do you subscribe to?
- ▶ What jobs have you enjoyed the most? The least? Why?
- ▶ What do you think determines an employee's progress in a good company?
- ▶ What qualifications do you have that make you feel you'll be successful in this field?

David Wesley, an EMT-Intermediate in San Diego, California, describes the EMT interviewing process as follows:

I wasn't very nervous during my interview. I knew I had the qualifications and initiative to do the job. Interviews today aren't as interrogative as they were 10 years ago. In some of the older EMT or firefighters' day, the interview was more like an interrogation because employers could get away with it. Now, there are many questions that are illegal, so it really comes down to qualifications and personality.

Asking Questions

Frequently, toward the close of an interview, the interviewer will provide the opportunity for you to ask questions. Don't ever say that you don't have any questions. This is your chance to set yourself apart from the competition. Prepare your questions in advance, and ask the most important questions first, in case there is not enough time to ask all of them. Do not ask questions that might show a lack of research. It is inappropriate to ask about salary and benefits unless the employer is offering you a position. Most employers do not want to discuss those issues until they are certain you are the right person for the job, so they will leave those issues for a second interview. Some examples of suitable questions are:

- ▶ What is the realistic time frame for advancement?
- ▶ How is an employee evaluated and promoted? Is it company policy to promote from within? Is there a probationary period?
- ▶ Tell me about your initial and future training programs.
- ▶ What are the challenging facets of the job?
- ▶ What are the opportunities for personal growth?
- ▶ What are this company's plans for future growth?
- ▶ What is this EMS company's record of employment stability?
- ▶ What makes your emergency service different from your competitors?
- ▶ What are this EMS company's strengths and weaknesses?
- ▶ How would you describe your EMS company's personality and management style?

Follow-up Strategy

Send a courtesy letter to thank each interviewer for the opportunity to speak with her or him. Mention the time and date of the original interview and any important points discussed. Include important qualifications that you may have omitted in the interview, and reiterate your interest in the job.

Do not be discouraged if a definite offer is not made at the interview or if a specific salary is not discussed. The interviewer will usually communicate with her or his office staff or interview other applicants before making an offer. Generally a decision is reached within a few weeks. Keep track of interviews on the calendar you are keeping to track your job search. Note the time period in which interviewers say you will hear from them. If you do not hear from them within that amount of time, follow up with a telephone call. However, you must show a commitment to their timetable. Don't call too soon or more than once.

You may not get the first job you apply for, if you are like most other EMTs. If this is the case, return to the beginning of the process and look again for available positions. Take stock of why you might not have been offered a job, too. If the reason(s) had to do with your interview skills, lack of training, or some other correctable item, work on it before applying again. Once you do land a job, you'll want to read Chapter 5 carefully for information about how to succeed.

INSIDE TRACK

Mary Ann Sanderson
Flight Paramedic
North Mississippi Medical Center
Tupelo, Mississippi

I have a degree in secondary education and I wanted to wait a few years before beginning teaching, so I went to work in a hospital business office. It was at that job that I was exposed to EMS personnel and decided to try it as a career. I began in 1984 as an EMT-Basic with a small, rural, hospital-based ambulance service.

I love the autonomy and the challenge of working in the prehospital environment, as well as helping people, both the patients as well as their families. Some of the things I dislike are the sometimes challenging physical and environmental stressors and having to be away from my family on holidays and other special occasions.

We work 12-hour shifts, and I never have a typical day, although I spend most of my time on training, quality assurance, and patient care. I may be in the office doing paperwork one minute and then get paged to respond to an MVC (motor vehicle collision) and spend the next two hours caring for patients. This includes anything from extrications to starting IVs and intubating to transporting a critical patient to a hospital. The day could end with some kind of public outreach and education, such as doing a helicopter PR program for a Cub Scout troop.

The profession is really maturing, as emergency medicine and prehospital care are changing every day. More quality people are joining the field and staying, rather than using EMS as a stepping stone to nursing or other medical fields. Now we're doing things in the field that were done only in the ER back when I began my career.

For people who want to enter EMS, it is important to learn about the reality—the TV version is not very realistic. Talk to people who have been in the field for a long time, and do some ride-alongs. And beware of the burned-out people out there—there are plenty of people who have been in EMS for years and still love the job and do it for the right reasons.

CHAPTER five

SUCCEEDING ON THE JOB

THIS CHAPTER shows how you can best succeed once you've begun your new career as an EMT. You'll find out how to become a top performer in EMS, learning the qualities that are rewarded, the procedures for moving up in the ranks, and the best ways to interact with coworkers and supervisors. You'll find examples of advancement opportunities within the EMS as well as alternative careers such as search-and-rescue unit, sales, and ski patrol careers. You'll also find helpful advice from EMT supervisors and EMTs who are already in the field.

YOU'VE GOTTEN your training, taken your exams, and become certified as an EMT. You have an understanding of an EMT's basic duties, but your training didn't cover how to manage work relationships or how to develop the qualities that are rewarded by supervisors and senior EMTs, fire chiefs, or police sergeants. There is much to learn regarding how to perform well on the job, beyond what you were taught in the classroom. Below we'll cover many of these topics, including promotion and advancement in your new field, so you'll be armed with the knowledge you need to succeed.

DEVELOPING THE QUALITIES THAT COUNT

When you are interviewed for an EMT position, your potential employer looks for qualities in your personality and on your resume that show you will be an asset to the EMS team. Even though you have enough of what it takes to get hired, after you begin your new position you may need to focus on those areas that you still need to develop. Working hard to obtain the qualities that spell success for an emergency care technician will not only improve your ability to do your job well, but gain the attention of your superiors as well. They'll see the dedication and seriousness that you apply to your career, which will help you later when it's time to think about getting promoted.

Be Alert

The most rewarded personal quality of an EMT is quick thinking, or mental alertness. EMTs receive emergency calls suddenly and unexpectedly, sometimes in the middle of the night, and they must be able to respond just as quickly. Knowing what to do in an emergency situation can mean the difference between a patient's life and death. If you rush through a call, you can falter in your judgment, possibly causing greater injury to the patient. A lack of mental alertness could even cost you your job as an EMT. Whether on an ambulance call, fire call, or police call, the choices you make have a profound impact on others. For this reason, the prehospital care community relies on drug screening tests, making sure all in their ranks are drug free. Even recreational drug use can significantly slow your response time and alter your thinking. To succeed as an EMT, you will need to do all you can to be physically and mentally in top shape; that means getting enough sleep, eating a healthy diet, and not engaging in habits that could adversely affect your quick-thinking skills.

Be Honest

Another rewarded personal quality of EMTs is honesty. Not only do your coworkers need to be able to trust you, but your patients do as well. This is the reason many police departments request that you see a psychologist and fire departments give scenario tests before hiring you as an EMT. EMT supervisors also question your honesty during an interview. Employers want to know what you would do in certain situations, and your answers can give them great insight into your character. You may be entrusted with a patient's belongings during a call, or be asked to testify in court about your team's response to an emergency. Everyone working with you, and those you are working for, need to know that you will be honest.

Be Calm

Successful EMTs are also able to remain calm in a crisis. If you appear stressed, the patient and his or her family are going to be even more concerned about the situation than they were already. You don't want to make a crisis situation worse by raising the anxiety level of those around you. It is therefore essential that you stay calm, reassuring the patient and any bystanders or family members, and remembering that they may not need to know everything about the victim's injuries at the scene. No matter how bad things might look right away, once a patient arrives at the hospital, care that often saves lives is available. Susan Carpenter, a volunteer EMT-B in Cary, North Carolina, explains this further:

> Every time the buzzer and pagers go off at the station, I get butterflies in my stomach. No two calls are ever the same. I think the day an EMT or paramedic doesn't get the butterflies is the day a mistake will happen. We deal with peoples' lives as well as distraught family members, and we need to stay calm. We must learn to be discreet and keep our mouths shut at appropriate times. These people are scared and need comfort and reassuring. We are there to help, not to make things worse.

Have a Sense of Humor

One of the most rewarded qualities of an EMT, whether working in an ambulance service, fire department, or other EMS facility, is having a sense of humor. A fire officer-EMT explains:

> Since most of our time spent in the fire station is downtime, waiting on calls, we spend a lot of time together just getting along. We have our daily duties, but mostly we have to be prepared to respond to any call. Many of the guys take to joking, cutting up over almost anything. If you can't take a joke, you won't like being in the midst of most discussions.

Humor is a very effective tool used to reduce stress. EMTs employ it to deal with the emergency situations they are involved in daily. Joking and kidding are also used to bond a group. Especially after you are first hired, your company may tease you as a way to test whether or not you will fit in. Another EMT explains her experiences:

> I found it hard to fit in at first, but a lot of that was that I was very nervous and anxious to learn. As a female in a mostly male world, as well as someone with no fire service background, it was a little harder to handle the guys at times. Get in the same room with four firefighter guys and guess at the topics. In general though, once you get over being new, it's not too hard to find your niche. Besides being able to take a joke, the qualities I see being rewarded by coworkers and supervisors include being a hard worker, reliable, safe, and willing to look for ways to get better at what we do.

Learn from Your Mistakes

Almost all EMTs will tell you that they need to be able to learn from mistakes and not to take criticism personally. Everyone makes mistakes, but successful people are able to learn from them and improve their skills. With each experience, you will gain a sharper eye and keener knowledge about how to react in each crisis. Your coworkers will help you through your mistakes as well. They will be able to see from another point of view exactly what went wrong, and offer constructive criticism to help you improve.

It is also important to stay open to learning new ways of doing things, in order to constantly improve your job performance. Just because you saved a life on your last call doesn't mean you won't be faced with a new challenge on the next. Robert Kagel, an EMT chief at Uwchlan Ambulance in Pennsylvania, adds:

> I have found that those EMTs who have an open mind and a willingness to listen to new ideas are the best EMTs. Be flexible. Know your stuff, and maintain a professional attitude and look. The one thing I can't stand as a supervisor and an EMT is a partner who does not maintain a high level of professionalism. You can know as much as you want; however, if you are unwilling to share that knowledge and maintain a professional look and attitude, I don't want to know you.

Have a Professional Appearance

It is immensely important to your career and your patients that you keep a professional appearance. Your appearance is important because it describes outwardly the type of person you are. Therefore you must maintain a high standard for personal grooming and uniform maintenance. You should always dress in the official uniform you receive from the EMS company or department that hired you. You may be given a uniform allowance, which can help maintain the uniforms you have or purchase new ones. Your uniform must always be clean and in good condition.

Be a Leader

Leadership qualities are necessary for those who wish to become officers; they must establish and maintain discipline and efficiency as well as direct the activities of EMTs in their companies. However, leadership qualities are also a plus for EMTs at any level.

When you are on a call, you need to be confident that you can handle every situation. You shouldn't have to depend on another team member to tell you what to do. If you can take charge in this manner, you have leadership qualities. You also need to be able to control the situation at the scene of an accident or crisis if there is no other help available, such as police or firefighters. You may be called upon to control a crowd or calm onlookers. This takes leadership skills as well.

Showing good leadership skills will also allow your supervisor to see your potential for promotion. Leaders take the time to share their knowledge with others, they take control in traumatic situations, and they are dependable in all working scenarios. These qualities will enhance your ability to move up the career ladder.

INTERACTING WITH PATIENTS

The way an EMT interacts with patients is extremely important. As mentioned previously, staying calm and projecting a professional attitude can help the patient and the patient's family members to stay calm. If you cannot remain levelheaded and calm under pressure, you could seriously upset the patient more than he or she already is, which can actually worsen a patient's condition. Bystanders or any family members who may be with the victim may also get more upset and excited if you cannot contain yourself. It is important as well that you do not describe the victim's circumstances in too much detail to the family, because the nature of injuries can change drastically once they have been treated at a hospital or medical facility.

If you work for an ambulance service, you may spend much of your time transporting patients. During this time you will need to call upon your professionalism and compassion. Many of your transported patients will be elderly and may need a friendly face to comfort them between locations, as well as an open ear to listen to them. No matter how tiresome or repetitive those in your care are, you need to respond with kindness.

Your professional attitude will come in handy with those patients who may be more difficult to handle than others. Some people become belligerent in a crisis, while other patients may have ongoing psychological problems that cause them to act out. Many times medications and difficult situations make patients uncomfortable, so they react in a negative way. There will also be instances when the patient is rude. You will need to be able to handle the situation without becoming rude yourself. Maintaining a professional demeanor in the face of unpleasant or volatile situations is a necessary part of an EMT's job.

INTERACTING WITH COWORKERS AND SUPERVISORS

The above-mentioned personal qualities are the same ones that your coworkers and supervisors will be looking for when you interact with them. Your employer will constantly check your abilities, your professional attitude, and how well you learn from your mistakes as a newly hired EMT. He or she will require you to be competent and knowledgeable, but most of all, dependable. Your coworkers will watch your job performance too, looking to see that you are like them, willing to go above and beyond the call of duty.

When interacting with coworkers and supervisors, you should be yourself and maintain a positive attitude. If you have been hired as an EMT, your supervisors have already determined that you have the right personality for the job. But you should avoid negativity, such as bad-mouthing anyone in your company. Don't show excessive pride, either. Bob Boyd, an EMT-Paramedic and fire chief from Bellingham, Washington, mentions that those who are in it for the glory won't last long. Remember that you became an EMT to help others by doing all you could to save their lives, and you will fit in with your coworkers and supervisors.

Your coworkers and supervisors are there to guide you and assist you at all times. However, don't take them for granted. Robert Kagel, EMT and assistant EMT chief, suggests:

> The best advice I can give about interacting with coworkers and supervisors is to stay away from the politics as much as possible. You have to respect your coworkers, even if you don't like a certain quality about them. Always be willing to learn from anyone you can, because no one knows everything. Someone is always teaching as someone is always learning. When interacting with your supervisors, just watch yourself. Be as flexible as possible. Also, if you help your supervisor out, he or she will in return help you, generally.

Another important aspect of getting along with coworkers and supervisors is getting to your shift on time. As mentioned above, EMTs must be dependable. If you arrive late, you may not have the time to receive or exchange any equipment you might need, and those who worked the shift before you will have to stay on the job longer, until you get there. Supervisors also care if you're late; it tells them that you cannot be depended on. If you are late for important emergency calls, you may make the difference between someone's life being saved and its not being saved.

LEARNING FROM MENTORS

Finding and learning from a mentor can be an essential element in your success. A mentor is someone you identify as successful and with whom you create an informal teacher-student relationship. Enter into the relationship intending to observe your mentor carefully, and ask questions. The following is a list of things you may learn from a mentor:

- ► public interaction skills
- ► how to study for promotion exams
- ► what to expect in the EMS culture
- ► how to communicate with the chain of command in your department
- ► in-depth knowledge about equipment and technology used by your department
- ► helpful tips for repair and maintenance of equipment and supplies

▶ which are the best EMT magazines and other resource materials

▶ what conferences/classes/training programs you should attend

You'll probably need to actively search for a mentor, unless someone decides to take you under his or her wing and show you the ropes. A mentor can be anyone from a battalion chief to one of your peers. There is no formula for who makes a good mentor; it is not based on title, level of seniority, or years in the department. Instead, the qualities of a good mentor are based on a combination of willingness to be a mentor, level of expertise in a certain area, teaching ability, and attitude.

When looking for a mentor, keep in mind the following questions:

▶ When asked a question, does the potential mentor take the time to help you find an answer rather than point you toward someone else who can help you?

▶ Does the potential mentor tackle problems in a reasonable manner until they are resolved?

▶ What is it that people admire about the potential mentor? Do the admirable qualities coincide with your values and goals?

▶ Is he or she strong in areas where you are weak?

Once you've entered into a relationship with a mentor, you should learn as much as you can from him or her. Keep in mind that, after a while, career growth may open up different possibilities in new areas of specialization. If that happens, you'll probably want to find additional mentors who can show you the ropes in the new environment. However, any former mentors you can keep as friends not only will help you careerwise, but also can enrich your life.

EVALUATIONS AND ON-THE-JOB TRAINING

As a new EMT, you will be evaluated after each call by the attending EMT in the ambulance with you. You will need to be able to check off an ambulance without assistance; this means that a person will test you by taking certain items off a fully loaded ambulance and asking you to tell him or her what is missing. You will be involved with on-the-job training almost the whole time you are an EMT, because, as EMT-Basic Susan Carpenter says, no two calls are ever the same.

IN THE NEWS

Emergency!

Never before has the prehospital care community been so well-represented on the small screen. From humble beginnings in the 1970s with *Emergency!* the networks have expanded the number of series that feature EMS workers, and these shows are more realistic than ever. They are so popular that a Website has been developed just to take the mystery out of medical terminology for faithful viewers. On www.geocities.com/TelevisionCity/5196/medspeak.html you can discover, among hundreds of terms mentioned in your favorite TV medical dramas, that *dyspnea* means "shortness of breath," heparin is a blood coagulant, and a "perfed appy" is when an infected appendix bursts open and spills into the gut.

PROFESSIONAL DEVELOPMENT

You will need to develop public relations and public speaking skills during your career as an EMT. These skills will be necessary when you find yourself interacting with reporters and public officials. You will need to know what to say and what not to say about the patients you aid, especially to reporters. For example, if you are at the scene of an automobile accident or other type of serious accident that involved young children, you would not offer the names of such victims to reporters until the family has been notified. These rules provide the victims with the confidentiality they deserve.

You'll also need these skills to interact effectively with coworkers. For example, you must relay all the circumstances of your patient's status upon entering the emergency room of a hospital or other medical facility. In addition, you will need to accurately describe vital signs to the nurses and doctors who will take over the care of the emergency victim.

There may also be times when you will give emergency and safety lectures to others, such as local elementary, middle school, or high school students who visit your EMS company. You may also give lectures as a guest speaker for an EMT adult education class or other related continuing education course. Such public speaking experiences can help prepare you for additional responsibilities and advancements in your future career. If you're promoted, you may need to interview other employment candidates or give daily shift meetings or briefings to go over the details of the upcoming shift. You can look at all of these ways of communicating as opportunities to improve your public speaking skills.

MAINTAINING PERSONAL HEALTH AND FITNESS

Another extremely important part of being an EMT is taking care of yourself, your body and your mind. You can't help others if you don't first take care of yourself. Getting enough sleep at night may be the single most important step you can take to protect your health and the health of your patients. If you're tired, you can't focus on the task at hand, and emergency victims need your full attention.

Eating a healthy diet is also an important way to maintain and protect your health. For example, eating a healthy breakfast can keep your attention away from hunger pains on your job. What you eat for breakfast or any other meal has an affect on your well-being. Eating burgers and fries for lunch and pizza for dinner has a slowing effect. Some people find that eating a light lunch and then taking a short walk immensely improves the quality of their workday afternoons.

Because of the demanding physical aspects of the job, EMTs must maintain a high level of fitness in order to continue to perform their duties at optimal levels. Regular exercise will do more than help with physical job duties, though; exercise has been shown to be an effective stress reducer and mood enhancer.

Protect yourself on the job by wearing protective gear such as gloves and eyewear when necessary. Just as firefighters are required to wear protective clothes to protect them from fire burns and smoke inhalation, EMTs must wear gloves to protect them from diseases that can be passed through blood and masks to protect them from diseases passed through the air. You may also be required to wear a protective jacket or overcoat to keep your clothes or uniform clean.

A seatbelt will be provided in the front seats of the ambulance as well as in the back seats. It will benefit your safety greatly to wear it, since the ambulance will be riding at high speeds. Fire trucks and engines also provide seatbelts, as do police cars and other safety vehicles. Remember that if you do not make it to the scene safely, you cannot save a victim's life.

KEEPING YOUR CERTIFICATION CURRENT

A few years after your initial certification, you will need to become recertified. Time requirements vary depending upon the state in which you are working, but expect to need recertification every two to four years.

Recertification usually requires a certain number of hours of continuing education, demonstration of your continuing ability to perform the necessary emergency medical skills, or both. The process assures that you are always on top of new technological advances and continuously honing your skills to be ready for all circumstances that evolve. Your certification tells your patients that you are capable of aiding them in an emergency situation.

Today, almost 80% of fire departments run by state and county communities require the firefighter-EMT to be certified at the time of employment, and the rest will require certification once you have joined the department. Police officers who are also EMTs must keep their certification current in order to be able to use AEDs and offer emergency medical services to victims. EMTs in all these professions are required to obtain further education on a regular basis to keep current with new technology and skills in the emergency medical field.

Lapsed Certification

To be reinstated once your EMT registration has lapsed, you must do one of the following:

- ▶ If it has lapsed within a two-year period, you must successfully complete a state-approved refresher course for whatever certification you had last. You must submit a new application and fee and successfully complete the state-approved test.
- ▶ If it lapsed more than two years ago, you may have to complete another EMT-Basic training course. If you were an EMT-Intermediate and your certification lapsed more than two years ago, you will have to document your successful completion of a state-approved EMT-Basic and EMT-

Intermediate training course, submit a new application and fee, and successfully pass a state-approved written and practical examination.

THE ROLE OF UNIONS

When you become an EMT, you may decide to join a labor union. A union combines strength and resources to organize for your rights as a laborer. There are many different types of unions for all kinds of workers. Depending on the region in which you work, unions may work to ensure that you receive the highest possible salary and benefits according to your level of experience. The union does many other things for its members, such as:

▶ providing training and retraining programs
▶ setting standards for health care workers and patient care
▶ improving conditions for workers, which improves the care given to patients
▶ developing leadership and advocacy skills in workers
▶ negotiating patient care contracts to address quality-of-care concerns
▶ negotiating increased wages, benefits, and pensions to curtail staff turnover
▶ working in coalition with health care reform advocates

Unions that represent EMTs include the International Association of Fire Fighters, which sponsor firefighter-EMTs, and the Service Employees Internet Union. More information about these and other unions can be found in Appendix B under the heading Professional Associations and Unions. Bill Boyd, a paramedic and fire captain from Bellingham, Washington, describes his union:

I'm a member of the International Association of Fire Fighters Local 106, and I am a strong believer in collective bargaining. We have a strong labor/management relationship that has resulted in excellent benefits, wages, and working conditions for our members. This probably would not have been possible without strong union support.

Particular areas of the country, such as the Northern states, encourage the formation of unions more than other areas do, through their state legislature. In the North, many ambulance services and fire departments require their employees to join a union in order to work for them. In many of these locations, unions are highly esteemed traditions. However, there are not as many union coalitions in the Southern states, which have legislation called the "right to work" that makes it harder for unions to organize. Also many small fire departments and ambulance services may not be affiliated with a particular union.

ADVANCEMENT OPPORTUNITIES

In order for an EMT-Basic to get a promotion, he or she must usually get additional training. However, it is possible to advance yourself to a better job without first getting certified at the next EMT level (Intermediate or Paramedic). Of course, at any level, if you wish to be considered for a promotion, you must perform your current job to the best of your abilities, showing your supervisor that you take your career seriously.

Promote Yourself to a Better Job

You can promote yourself to a better job by getting hired as an EMT in another EMS company that offers you more advancement opportunities. There are several reasons why you might want to apply to another prehospital care company. Even if it's a lateral move, you might get any one or more of the following added benefits from a move:

► better pay
► better health benefits or work schedule
► better training programs
► better EMS equipment
► better camaraderie with coworkers and supervisors
► more room for advancement

These potential benefits usually don't apply to those whose first job is with a large company that offers highly competitive salaries and other bonuses, as well as many opportunities for advancement. In such a case, focus on learning all you can and on applying yourself for future promotional opportunities or career challenges in related areas at that company. If you decide to seek advancement in the EMS field, there are several things you can do to prepare for a promotion.

How to Prepare for a Promotion

Many experienced EMTs study regularly to improve their job performance and prepare for promotion examinations. Today, EMTs at all levels need more training to operate increasingly sophisticated equipment and deal safely with the greater hazards associated with emergency situations such as fighting fires, controlling criminals, and stabilizing severely injured victims.

To progress to higher-level positions, EMTs must acquire expertise in the most advanced EMT equipment and lifesaving techniques and emergency procedures, as well as in writing, public speaking, management and budgeting procedures, and labor relations. This is true for all EMT-Basics who want to become EMT-Intermediates or EMT-Paramedics, as well as for firefighter-EMTs who want to be promoted within the fire department or police officer-EMTs who want to be promoted within the police department.

Acquiring advanced certifications is one way in which to make yourself stand out from your peers and ready yourself for a promotion. These certifications are explained in greater detail in Chapter 2. They include advanced cardiac life support (ACLS), basic trauma life support (BTLS), and pediatric advanced life support (PALS), among others. Sometimes these advanced certification courses are offered as part of an EMT-Intermediate or EMT-Paramedic training program, and they are also offered separately at EMS training schools, community and technical colleges, and other institutions.

IN THE NEWS

EMTs in the Mosh Pit

EMTs get the chance to hang out and listen to music while they work; concerts where "mosh pits" are popular have traumatic injury rates over 10 times those of "nonmoshing" shows, and EMTs are in high demand at these events. A "mosh pit" is an area, often directly in front of the stage, where people are tightly packed together amidst wild and often violent dancing, stage divers dropping down into the crowd, and crowd surfers being passed from hand to hand overhead. Injuries to mosh pit participants are usually to the head, cervical spine, and extremities, all of which are areas that demand skilled and immediate medical attention such as is provided by professional EMTs.

Taking the Promotional Exam

There are several things you can do to improve your chances of scoring high on a promotional exam.

▶ Get an idea of what will be on the promotional exam. Ask those who have already taken the exam what areas were emphasized and what books they recommend you study to prepare for the exam. You may also be able to get old tests that have been published for students to review relevant material. In some departments, although this is rare, you may be fortunate enough to get a suggested reading list along with the exam materials.

▶ Study test preparation books to find out or brush up on the skills needed to succeed on promotional exams and to take practice exams. For example, look up information on how to handle test anxiety, how to score as high as possible on multiple-choice questions, and how to take tests within specific time limits.

▶ Make a study schedule several months before the exam, and stick to it. Allow sufficient time each day for studying a section of material, and don't forget to preview and review the material you study each day. One study method is to create flash cards and test yourself on key concepts and questions that you think might appear on the test.

▶ Find out if your EMS company uses assessment centers to test practical, hands-on aspects of the job you are applying for. If so, talk to people who have gone through the assessment center to get their advice on how you can prepare for this part of the process. You should also ask if you can tour the assessment facility to get an idea of what equipment is used for testing.

Promotion to EMT-Paramedic

Many hospitals want EMTs to be paramedics or to be enrolled in paramedic training, because EMT-Paramedics can perform more advanced prehospital procedures, such as administering drugs intravenously, performing endotracheal intubations, and operating complicated life support equipment. This career advancement can raise your salary about $10,000 a year.

Opportunities for EMT-Basics or EMT-Intermediates who receive this advanced training while working in small ambulance services, fire departments, or police departments often depend on the status of senior EMTs in the particular department or on turnover rates. For example, in many small emergency medical facilities, EMTs must wait until someone leaves the company before they get a promotion.

Turnover rates for EMT-Basics and EMT-Intermediates are higher in the private-service sector than in the public-service sector due to stressful working conditions, limited advancement potential, and modest pay and benefits. Therefore opportunities for entry-level EMTs are better in hospitals and private ambulance services, where pay and benefits are usually lower. Many EMTs get their start in the private sector and then move into the public sector once they have achieved a certain level of experience.

Below is an example of a recent job posting for an EMT-Paramedic, to give you an idea of what advancement opportunities are available in your future career.

Job Summary	EMT-Paramedic
Education	Completion of EMT-Paramedic program
Licensure	Current state or NREMT certification as EMT-Paramedic; current CPR and ACLS certification

Experience	Three years of high-performance EMS experience preferred
Skills	Applicant must possess skills related to experience as EMT-Paramedic
Essential Physical and Mental Functions and Environmental Conditions	Applicant must be able to communicate effectively with patients, dispatchers, and medical facility staff.
	Applicant must be able to care adequately for patients under the guidelines of the title EMT-Paramedic
	Applicant must be able to handle traumatic situations calmly and efficiently and remain in control under extreme duress
	Applicant must provide a clean driving record, background record, drug screen, and excellent physical examination

Promotion in the Fire Department

Opportunities for promotion are good in most fire departments. As fire-fighter-EMTs gain expertise, they may advance to a higher rank. The line of promotion is usually to engineer, lieutenant, captain, battalion chief, assistant chief, deputy chief, and, finally, chief. For EMT-Basics, it may be to the EMT-Intermediate or EMT-Paramedic position. Advancement generally depends upon written examination scores, job performance, interviews, and seniority. Increasingly, fire departments are using assessment centers, which simulate a variety of actual job performance tasks—to screen for the best candidates for promotion.

Associate's and bachelor's degrees are available in fire science as well as EMT-Paramedic. Many fire departments now require a bachelor's degree—preferably in fire science, public administration, or a related field—for promotion to positions higher than battalion chief. Some departments also require a master's degree, as well as executive fire officer certification from the National Fire Academy or state chief officer certification, for the position of fire chief.

Below is a recent job posting for a Firefighter II/Paramedic, giving you an idea of the advancement opportunities available in the fire-fighting EMS field.

Position	Firefighter II/Paramedic
Education	Completed EMT-Paramedic certificate and Firefighter I certificate courses; college degree preferred
Licensure	Current state or NREMT EMT-Paramedic certification; ACLS, PALS, PHTLS/BTLS, Firefighter II; NWCG Red Card preferred
Experience	Three years as a professional firefighter
Skills	Skills must be related to fire fighting and EMT-Paramedic status
Essential Physical and Mental Functions and Environmental Conditions	Qualified candidates must be between the ages of 21 and 35
	Applicants must be able to handle heavy emphasis on wildland fire fighting and technical rescue
	Applicants must be able to communicate effectively with fire officers, dispatchers, medical professionals, and accident victims
	Applicants must be able to complete necessary fire drills, drive emergency vehicles, and use necessary fire and EMT equipment

Promotion in the Police Department

Police officers usually become eligible for promotion after a probationary period ranging from six months to three years. Promotion may consist of moving from Police Officer I to Police Officer II and so on before moving up to corporal, sergeant, lieutenant, and captain. These promotions are usually made according to a candidate's position on a promotion list as determined by written promotion examination scores, referrals, and on-the-job performance.

There is also a growing trend for police departments to hire and promote those with at least some college credits, even if the courses are not directly related to police work. Required continued training and refresher courses aid officers in improving their job performance.

Review the following example of a recent job posting for Police Officer/Paramedic to get an idea of the advancement opportunities available in emergency medical services in police departments.

Job Summary	Police officer/Paramedic
Education	Completed police officer academy training courses; completed EMT-Paramedic certificate course or associate degree course
Licensure	Current state or NREMT EMT-Paramedic certification; current CPR and ACLS certification
Experience	At least two years as a street paramedic
Skills	Applicant must possess skills related to the police officer and the EMT-Paramedic
Essential Physical and Mental Functions and Environmental Conditions	Applicant must be at least 21 years of age, in excellent physical and mental health, and be able to remain in control under extreme duress
	Applicant must be able to recall details of the scenes of crimes, preserve evidence as appropriate, and secure the safety of the emergency scene using investigation and identification techniques
	Applicant must be able to provide emergency relief to victims of emergencies, utilize necessary equipment, and cooperate with local EMS agencies
	Applicant must be able to communicate with victims, bystanders, and dispatchers and provide crowd control

RELATED CAREER OPTIONS

There are many different career options available for EMTs. As discussed previously, you can receive additional training and advance through the levels of EMT certification and/or get promoted within your company or by making a move to another company. There also exist a number of alternative employment opportunities that you can consider. Below we detail a number of careers that are related to or use the experience gained through EMS work.

EMT Dispatcher

EMTs can, with further training, become EMT dispatchers. As discussed in Chapter 1, the dispatcher receives the call for help, sends out the appropriate medical resource, remains the link between the emergency vehicle and the medical facility throughout the situation, and relays any requests for special assistance to the hospital. Dispatchers are crucial in helping EMTs get to the scene of an accident. Dispatchers also play a key role in helping to save the lives of medical emergency victims. They may need to give lifesaving instructions to bystanders or family members while the victims are awaiting an ambulance or other emergency units.

A dispatcher usually holds EMT-Intermediate or EMT-Paramedic certification and may be required to have ACLS, BTLS or PHTLS, PPPC, NALS, or PALS. He or she must receive training and show proficiency in the use of state-of-the-art technology. Larger EMS companies in urban areas can receive 750,000 calls or more per year, making the job of dispatcher fast-paced in addition to being the vital link between patient and emergency care.

Instructor

EMT-Paramedics can become instructors of EMT courses, teaching others their skills and sharing their years of experience. You can become an instructor at whatever level of EMT training you achieve, notes Jeanine Hoffman, EMT-Basic, class coordinator, and primary instructor at Harrisburg Community College in Pennsylvania. A college or technical institute you wish to teach at may have special requirements, such as possession of an associate's or bachelor's degree or a certain number of years of experience.

You may also teach classes outside of a school or technical institute atmosphere. For example, many EMS companies give CPR, first aid, and other types of safety classes. EMS companies may also be the site of EMT-Basic and EMT-Intermediate refresher courses.

Salaries for instructors depend greatly on academic credentials, experience, and the region of the country in which you are teaching. You may become a full-time or part-time instructor, teaching while working or volunteering as an EMT. Whatever path you choose, becoming an instructor is a great way to pass on the wealth of experience and knowledge you gain as an EMT.

Flight Paramedic

EMT-Paramedics can become flight paramedics for emergency air medical transport, and those with a pilot's license can fly the small planes or helicopters used for the transport. Airplanes and helicopters routinely fly critical-care patients from one medical facility to another, and they also move patients who may be unable to fly on commercial airlines for any number of reasons. Flight paramedicine is often an expanded role for paramedics. It can be challenging, rewarding, and highly competitive.

For more information on becoming a flight paramedic, look up the National Flight Paramedics Association website, www.nfpa.rotor.com; you can also write to the association at 383 F Street, Salt Lake City, UT 84103, or call 800-381-NFPA.

Search-and-Rescue Unit

EMTs can train to work on search-and-rescue units that are all-terrain, all-weather, ground, air, water, mountain, and disaster relief teams. Unit members are trained in wilderness penetration and movement, land navigation, downed aircraft reconnaissance, lost-person search techniques, tracking strategies, wilderness rescue skills, team organization, water crossing, and wildfire suppression. These teams may also use search dogs to find victims.

Each team member is trained at minimum as a first responder or EMT-Basic, depending upon the requirements of the individual search-and-rescue team. Members are also certified in wildfire control, and units are capable of fielding certified divers for water search and rescue. Each geographical area may have a different kind of team, depending on the region's predominant land description. Search-and-rescue units in mountainous regions perform more cliff rescues and have more technical rope teams, whereas river regions require search-and-rescue teams trained in water rescue. Appropriate training is available in the different regions.

For more information on how to get hired and excel on search-and-rescue teams, see the National Association for Search and Rescue's website, www.nasar.org; contact the association at 4500 Southgate Place, Suite 100, Chantilly, VA 20151-1714; or call 703-222-6277. Other resources you can contact include

▶ The National Institute for Urban Search and Rescue: http://niusr.org; PO Box 91648, Santa Barbara, CA 93190; 805-569-5066
▶ The Mountain Rescue Association; www.mra.org: 710 Tenth Street, Suite 105, Golden, CO 80401; fax 503 658-6942
▶ The National Search and Rescue School: www2.acc.af.mil/afrccl/nss/index.html; USCG Training Center, Yorktown, VA 23690-5000; 757-856-2273

American Red Cross Worker

American Red Cross workers provide relief to victims of disasters and help people prevent, prepare for, and respond to emergencies. The American Red Cross provides many services, such as:

▶ food and shelter for victims of disasters
▶ services to members of the Armed Forces and their families

▶ instruction in first aid and water safety
▶ HIV/AIDS education
▶ home nursing
▶ blood and tissue banking services
▶ international aid

The work of the Red Cross is performed by over 1.5 million volunteers across the country, 30,000 staff members, and the financial contributions of the American people. There are 50 volunteers for every paid staff member. The Red Cross is committed to making a positive difference by improving the quality of human life, enhancing self-reliance and concern for others, and helping people avoid, prepare for, and cope with emergencies.

For more information about the American Red Cross and how you can volunteer, contact the American Red Cross at its national headquarters at 8111 Gatehouse Road, Falls Church, VA 22042, or at 431 18th Street NW, Washington, DC 20006; call 202-639-3520, or visit its website, www.red-cross.org.

Ski Patrol Unit

EMTs can also train to work on ski patrol units that serve skiers, hikers, snowboarders, and other snow- and mountain-stranded victims. Patrollers in ski patrol units are well-versed in various special rescue techniques including toboggan handling, chairlift evacuation, technical rope rescues, avalanche control and rescue, and out-of-area search-and-rescue.

Ski patrollers are usually certified as outdoor emergency care technicians. The requirement for obtaining this level of certification is completion of the EMT-Basic course work with an emphasis on patrolling the snow and mountain environment. Many colleges located close to geographic areas that get a lot of snow offer a course entitled Ski Area Operations as well as EMT and first responder courses. One is the Colorado Mountain College, which has campuses all over the state of Colorado. Another is the Center for Prehospital Care at UCLA (www.cpc.mednet.ucla.edu). On page 155 is a sample quiz given to students studying to become outdoor emergency care technicians.

Ski patrol units also offer safety programs to winter recreation participants. Such programs offer survival skills in areas such as emergency shelter construction, navigation by map, winter route planning, emergency equipment repair, and winter first aid.

For more information on ski patrol units, visit the National Ski Patrol's website, www.nsp.org; write to the patrol at 133 South Van Gordon Street, Suite 100, Lakewood, CO 80228; or call 303-988-1111.

Outdoor Emergency Care Pop Quiz

1. List five characteristics of a pulse or respiration.

2. What is a sign? Give an example.

3. What is a symptom? Give an example.

4. What does the pneumatic BSI stand for?

5. When is a patient considered unresponsive?

6. List the primary systems.

7. List three objectives of the patient assessment.

8. Your classmate's pulse and blood pressure are _____ and _____.

9. True or false:

    _____If someone refuses help, let him or her ski away and try not to make a big deal out of his or her refusal.

10. Describe where the following organs are located in the body:

    a. Spleen

    b. Heart

    c. Liver

    d. Appendix

    e. Kidneys

Nurse

EMTs may also enter the nursing field, moving from medical transport to the hospital to work as registered nurses (RNs), licensed practical nurses (LPNs), and nurse's aides. Unlike emergency medicine, where patient care is traumatic and short-term, nursing is more personal and long-term. EMT-Basics and EMT-Intermediates usually require more training to become an RN because becoming an RN requires an associate's or higher degree.

However, most EMT-Paramedics can switch over to nursing more easily, since they have probably already obtained an associate's degree. Becoming a nurse's aide would require almost no further training for any level EMT.

Many times EMTs feel that the stress of working in emergency services is taking a toll on their health, and they see a more calm and attractive environment in being a hospital or staff nurse caring for patients.

For more information about becoming a nurse, contact the American Nurses Association at 600 Maryland Avenue SW, Suite 100 West, Washington, DC 20024, call 800-274-4ANA, or visit the assoication's website, www.nursingworld.org. You might also want to contact:

▶ The National League for Nursing: www.nln.org; 350 Hudson Street, New York, NY 10014; 800-669-1656
▶ The Emergency Nurses Association: www.ena.org; 915 Lee Street, Des Plains, IL 60016-6569; 800-900-9659

Lifeguard

Lifeguard responsibilities include water rescue of swimmers and surfers, boater rescue up to three miles offshore, boat fire suppression, coastal cliff rescue, underwater search-and-rescue, missing persons, and other such related emergencies. Included within the lifeguard service is the boating safety unit that provides harbor patrol and ocean rescue service for boaters. Lifeguards assigned to a boating safety unit enforce boating regulations, and they handle the issuance of boat mooring permits and long-term boat beaching permits. During periods of flooding, lifeguard river rescue teams handle flood rescues. Dive rescue teams handle underwater search and recovery. Administrative positions may include a lifeguard chief, several lieutenants and sergeants, and an office staff.

Usually all full-time lifeguards are EMTs. Hourly lifeguards are certified by a minimum of American Red Cross Emergency Response. River rescue teams are certified at the instructor level. Dive rescue team members are certified as advanced scuba divers and dive rescue specialists. Lifeguards who work in boating safety units are fully equipped and trained to operate the lifeguard service's fire boats, and they also suppress fires.

For more career information on becoming a lifeguard, contact the United States Lifesaving Association at PO Box 366, Huntington Beach, CA 92648; visit its website, www.usla.com; or call 732-775-6449.

Sales Representative

EMT-Paramedics can become sales representatives, selling emergency medical equipment to EMS facilities. Manufacturers and wholesale sales representatives spend much of their time traveling to and visiting with prospective buyers and current clients. During a sales call, they discuss the customer's needs and suggest how their merchandise or services can meet those needs. They may show samples or catalogs that describe items their company stocks and inform customers about prices, availability, and how their products can save money and improve productivity. They also take orders and resolve any problems with or complaints about the merchandise.

Sales representatives usually cover large territories, and spend a considerable amount of time traveling. They may cover several states and be away from home for days or weeks at a time. However, they do have the freedom to determine their own schedule. Sales representatives also attend EMS trade shows to keep abreast of new merchandise and the changing needs of EMS customers.

Sales earnings vary significantly and are based either on commission and salary or commission and bonuses. Bonuses can be based on individual performance, on that of all the workers in a company, or on the company's performance. Sales representatives are usually reimbursed for expenses such as transportation costs, meals, hotels, and entertaining customers. They often receive benefits such as health and life insurance, a pension plan, vacation and sick leave, personal use of a company car, and frequent flier mileage.

On the Job

Anaphylaxis

Anaphylaxis is a rare, severe allergic reaction that is potentially life threatening. The most common causes of anaphylaxis include drugs such as penicillin, insect stings, foods, X-ray dye, latex, and exercise. The symptoms of anaphylaxis may vary from hives, tongue swelling, and vomiting, to shock. EMTs respond to anaphylaxis by injecting the patient with epinephrine; they may also use a tourniquet in cases of insect stings, to place a barrier between the puncture site and the heart. CPR may also be necessary, as anaphylaxis can stop a patient's heartbeat and breathing.

Software Engineers

Some EMTs move on to become software engineers, since they know first-hand the kind of software needed by an EMS company. For example, an EMT from Georgia created mapping software that is used by several hospitals and EMS facilities in the area. The software is used to more quickly locate the scene of an accident, as well as to locate the ambulances that are out on the road already. For some emergencies, it may be quicker to send an ambulance that is already out on the road returning from another call than to issue a new departure from the hospital or EMS facility. The mapping software is a more efficient way of viewing a map; it focuses on the scene of the emergency and the surrounding streets, and it offers suggestions on the best way to get there.

Software engineers are involved in the design and development of software systems that control and automate manufacturing, business, and management processes. They also may design and develop both packaged and systems software or be involved in creating custom software applications for clients.

Employers in this field generally look for people who are familiar with programming languages and who have a broad knowledge of and experience with computer systems and technologies. Successful software engineers also have strong problem-solving and analysis skills and good interpersonal skills. Taking courses in computer programming or systems design can offer you preparation for a job in this field.

For more information on becoming a software engineer, search the Internet using a search engine such as Google.com or Yahoo.com and the search term "emergency medical services software." You will get a list of companies, such as EMT Software, that develop and market such software. Visit their websites, many of which include job postings. Two to try are www.emtsoft.com and www.pinpointtech.com.

JUST THE FACTS

EMS and the Vietnam War

The Highway Safety Act of 1966 established the emergency medical services Program in the Department of Transportation. In 1973 The Emergency Medical Services Systems (EMSS) Act established additional federal guidelines and funding for the development of regional EMS systems. Both of these pieces of legislation were spurred by the realization that the emergency care provided to soldiers in Vietnam could serve as a model for a similar level of care in civilian populations.

ACHIEVING SUCCESS

You've worked hard to land your first job as an EMT. You received the proper training, studied for and took your exams, and achieved certification. Then you mounted a job search and went through the selection process before being offered a position. Now that you're on the job, you want to do your best to succeed. Make positive relationships with coworkers, share ideas and common interests, and maintain a positive attitude. Get to work on time, be efficient, and perform your job with the highest level of professionalism.

Find someone within your work environment to take you under his or her wing. Focus on maintaining a good work record after you've proven your capabilities during your probationary period. Show everyone your best, and you will have the chance to succeed and move on to larger environments and higher levels of pay. Also remember the EMT oath.

The EMT Oath

Be it pledged as an Emergency Medical Technician, I will honor the physical and judicial laws of God and man. I will follow that regimen which, according to my ability and judgment, I consider for the benefit of patients and abstain from whatever is deleterious and mischievous, nor shall I suggest any such counsel. Into whatever homes I enter, I will go into them for the benefit of only the sick and injured, never revealing what I see or hear in the lives of men unless required by law.

I shall also share my medical knowledge with those who may benefit from what I have learned. I will serve unselfishly and continuously in order to help make a better world for all mankind.

While I continue to keep this oath unviolated, may it be granted to me to enjoy life, and the practice of the art, respected by all men, in all times. Should I trespass or violate this oath, may the reverse be my lot.

So help me God.

INSIDE TRACK

Veronica Ann Gahgan
Paramedic
Bonnie Brook Fire Protection District, Illinois

I used to love the reruns of *Emergency* when I was growing up. I would carry around a tackle box full of Band-Aids and gauze. All I wanted to do was help people in trouble, and when I was 18, I began working with a few private ambulances as an EMT-A, which is a certification level that no longer exists. I also did a lot of ride-alongs with a local fire department which then sponsored me for paramedic school, and now here I am in my eighth year in EMS, a career that I enjoy!

I like helping people in general, and the best part of the work to me is not necessarily the skills I provide, but the chance to truly interact with people and treat the person as a whole. The EMS field has so much potential to be more than just providing immediate care. By far the most troublesome part of EMS work is the calls involving children. I have seen more awful things in eight years than most people will ever see in their lifetime. While you're on the call it's not a big deal, because you just do what you need to do and what you have been trained to do, but after it's over and you have a chance to think, it can hit you really hard. Thankfully here in Illinois we are offered critical incident stress debriefing to assist us with handling our feelings. EMS can truly burn you out quickly if you don't know how to deal with what you feel.

We are a part-time/paid-on-call department in an area with many full-time departments. We have a lot of responsibilities besides actual emergency care, such as station maintenance, logging calls, public education, and public outreach, but when these duties are completed and there aren't any calls, the time is ours to do with as we please. Many people use this time to read or study.

The scope of what is being taught and what EMTs are authorized to do is expanding rapidly. The EMT curriculum is being worked into college degree programs, which means more study of basic anatomy and a better working knowledge of the body. The equipment is also much more advanced, along with constant development and implementation of new protocols, and survival rates are improving because of all of these factors.

If you truly like to help people, then a career as an EMT is one of the best ways to do it. You will probably spend more time waiting for the calls than actually going out on them, you won't make a million dollars, and most of the time, you won't even get a thank-you. But if you can take satisfaction in knowing that you did the best you could to help, you will enjoy this career.

APPENDIX A

Employment Resources

STATE EMS AGENCIES

ALABAMA

Alabama Department of Public Health, EMS
  Division
RSA Tower
201 Monroe Street, Suite 750
Montgomery, AL 36104
800-962-9234, 334-206-5383
www.alapubhealth.org

ALASKA

Community Health and Emergency Medical
  Services Program
Alaska Department of Health and Social
  Services, Division of Public Health
410 Willoughby, Room 109
Box 110616
Juneau, AL 99811-0616
907-465-3027
www.chems.alaska.gov

ARIZONA

Bureau of Emergency Medical Services
Arizona Department of Health Services
1651 East Morten
Phoenix, AZ 85020
800-200-8523, 602-861-0708
www.hs.state.az.us/bems/index.htm

ARKANSAS

Division of Emergency Medical Services and
  Trauma Systems, Bureau of Health
  Resources
Arkansas Department of Health
4815 West Markham Street, Slot 38
Little Rock, AR 72205
501-661-2262
http://health.state.ar.us/index.html

CALIFORNIA

Emergency Medical Services Authority
1930 Ninth Street
Sacramento, CA 95814
916-322-4336
www.emsa.cahwnet.gov

COLORADO

Emergency Medical Services Division
Colorado Department of Health
4300 Cherry Creek Drive South, 5th Floor
Glendale, CO 80246-1530
303-692-2980
www.cdphe.state.co.us/em/emhom.html

CONNECTICUT

Office of Emergency Medical Services

Department of Public Health

410 Capitol Avenue

Hartford, CT 06134-0308

860-509-7975

www.state.ct.us/dph/BRS/EMS_Office/
  ems.htm

DELAWARE

Delaware Office of Emergency Medical
  Services

655 Bay Road, Suite 4H

Dover, DE 19901

302-739-4710

www.state.de.us/dhss/dph/ems

DISTRICT OF COLUMBIA

Emergency Health and Medical Services

D.C. Department of Health

825 North Capitol Street, NE, Room 4177

Washington, DC 20002

202-442-9111

www.dchealth.com/ehms/welcome.htm

FLORIDA

Bureau of Emergency Medical Services

Florida Department of Health

4052 Bald Cypress Way, Mail Bin C18

Tallahassee, FL 32399-1738

850-245-4440

www.doh.state.fl.us

GEORGIA

Office of Emergency Medical Services

Georgia Division of Public Health

The Skyland Center, Lower Level

2600 Skyland Drive

Atlanta, GA 30319

404-679-0547

www.ph.dhr.state.ga.us/programs/ems/index
  .shtml

HAWAII

State Emergency Medical Services System

Hawaii Department of Health

3627 Kilauea Avenue, Room 102

Honolulu, HI 96816-2317

808-733-9210

IDAHO

Bureau of Emergency Medical Services

Department of Health and Welfare

450 West State Street

Boise, ID 83720-0036

208-334-5500

www2.state.id.us/dhw/hwgd_www/
  organiza/Directory/health.htm

ILLINOIS

Division of Emergency Medical Services

Illinois Department of Public Health

525 West Jefferson Street, 3rd Floor

Springfield, IL 62761

217-785-2080

www.idph.state.il.us

INDIANA

Indiana Emergency Medical Services
   Commission
State Emergency Management Agency
302 West Washington, Room E239 IGCS
Indianapolis, IN 46204
317-233-6545
www.ai.org/sema/ems.html

IOWA

Bureau of Emergency Medical Services
Iowa Department of Public Health
Lucas State Office Building
321 East Twelfth Street
Des Moines, IA 50319-0075
800-728-3367
http://idph.state.ia.us/pa/ems/default.htm

KANSAS

Board of Emergency Medical Services
109 SW Sixth Avenue
Topeka, KS 66603-3826
785-296-7296
www.ksbems.org

KENTUCKY

Emergency Medical Services Branch
Department for Health Services
275 East Main Street
Frankfort, KY 40621
502-564-3970
http://publichealth.state.ky.us/ems.htm

LOUISIANA

Emergency Medical Services
Division of Community Health
Office of Public Health
Department of Health and Hospitals
161 Third Street
Baton Rouge, LA 70801
225-342-4881
www.dhh.state.la.us/oph/progsvc.htm

MAINE

Bureau of Emergency Medical Services
Department of Public Health
16 Edison Drive
Augusta, ME 04330
207-287-3953
http://janus.state.me.us/dps/ems/
   homepage.htm

MARYLAND

The Maryland Institute for Emergency
   Medical Services Systems
653 West Pratt Street
Baltimore, MD 21201-1536
410-706-5074
http://miemss.umaryland.edu/Home.htm

MASSACHUSETTS

Office of Emergency Medical Services
Department of Public Health
56 Roland Street
Boston, MA 02129
617-284-8300
www.state.ma.us/dph/oems

MICHIGAN

Division of Emergency Medical Services

Department of Consumer and Industry Affairs

525 West Ottawa

Lansing, MI 48909

517-373-1820

www.cis.state.mi.us/bhs/hfs/ems/
   emshome.htm

MINNESOTA

Minnesota Emergency Service Regulatory
   Board

2829 University Avenue Southeast, Suite 310

Minneapolis, MN 55414-3222

612-627-6000

www.emsrb.state.mn.us

MISSISSIPPI

Emergency Medical Services Division

Mississippi State Department of Health

PO Box 1700

Jackson, MS 39215-1700

601-576-7380

www.msdh.state.ms.us/ems/index.htm

MISSOURI

Bureau of Emergency Medical Services

Missouri Department of Health

912 Wildwood

Jefferson City, MO 65109

573-751-6356

www.health.state.mo.us/EMS

MONTANA

Emergency Medical Services and Injury
   Prevention Section

Department of Public Health and Human
   Services

PO Box 202951

Helena, MT 59620

406-444-3895

www.dphhs.state.mt.us/hpsd/pubheal/
   healsafe/ems

NEBRASKA

Emergency Medical Services Program

Department of Health and Human Services

301 Centennial Mall South, 3rd Floor

Lincoln, NE 68509-5007

402-471-2299

www.hhs.state.ne.us/ems/emsindex.htm

NEVADA

Emergency Medical Services Office

Nevada State Health Division

1550 East College Parkway, Suite 158

Carson City, NV 89706

775-687-3065

http://health2k.state.nv.us/ems/index.htm

NEW HAMPSHIRE

Division of Emergency Medical Services

New Hampshire Department of Safety

10 Hazen Drive

Concord, NH 03305

603-271-4568

www.state.nh.us/safety/ems

NEW JERSEY

Office of Emergency Medical Services

New Jersey Department of Health and
Senior Services

PO Box 360

Trenton, NJ 08525-0360

609-633-7777

www.state.nj.us/health/ems/hlthems.htm

NEW MEXICO

Injury Prevention and Emergency Medical
Services Bureau

2500 Cerrillos Road

Santa Fe, NM 87505

505-476-7701

www.health.state.nm.us/website.nsf/WebNav
Lookup/4457DE9ED75DE80A8725673C
0059F990?OpenDocument

NEW YORK

Bureau of Emergency Medical Services

New York State Department of Health

433 River Street, Suite 303

Troy, NY 12180-2299

518-402-0996

www.health.state.ny.us/nysdoh/search/
index.htm

NORTH CAROLINA

Office of Emergency Medical Services

Division of Facility Services

2707 Mail Service Center

Raleigh, NC 27699-2707

919-733-2285

www.ncems.org

NORTH DAKOTA

Division of Emergency Health Services

North Dakota Department of Health

600 East Boulevard Avenue

Bismarck, ND 58505-0200

701-328-2388

www.health.state.nd.us/ndhd/resource/dehs/
dehs.htm

OHIO

Division of Emergency Medical Services

Ohio Department of Public Safety

PO Box 182073

1970 West Broad Street

Columbus, OH 43218-2073

800-233-0785

www.state.oh.us/odps/division/ems/
ems_local/default.htm

OKLAHOMA

Emergency Medical Services Division

State Department of Health

1000 NE 10th Street, Room 1104

Oklahoma City, OK 73117-1299

405-271-4027

www.health.state.ok.us

OREGON

Emergency Medical Services and Systems

Oregon Health Division

Department of Human Services

Portland State Office Building

800 NE Oregon Street

Portland, OR 97232

503-731-4000

www.ohd.hr.state.or.us/ems/welcome.htm

PENNSYLVANIA

Emergency Medical Services Office

Pennsylvania Department of Health

PO Box 90

Harrisburg, PA 17108

717-787-8741

www.health.state.pa.us/hpa/ems

RHODE ISLAND

Division of Emergency Medical Services

Department of Health, Room 105

3 Capitol Hill

Providence, RI 02908

401-222-2401

www.health.state.ri.us

SOUTH CAROLINA

Emergency Medical Services

Department of Health and Environmental
    Control

2600 Bull Street

Columbia, SC 29201

803-737-7204

www.state.sc.us/dhec/NewEMS/index.htm

SOUTH DAKOTA

Emergency Medical Services

South Dakota Department of Health

600 East Capitol

Pierre, SD 57501-2536

605-773-4031

www.state.sd.us/doh/EMS/index.htm

TENNESSEE

Division of Emergency Medical Services

Tennessee Department of Health

425 Fifth Avenue North, 1st Floor, Room 88

Nashville, TN 37247-0701

615-741-2584

www.state.tn.us/health

TEXAS

Bureau of Emergency Management

Texas Department of Health

1100 West 49th Street

Austin, TX 78756-3199

512-834-6700

www.tdh.state.tx.us/hcqs/ems/emshome.htm

UTAH

Bureau of Emergency Medical Services

Utah Department of Health

PO Box 142004

Salt Lake City, UT 84114-2004

801-538-6435

http://hlunix.hl.state.ut.us/ems

VERMONT

EMS and Injury Prevention

Division of Health Protection

Vermont Department of Health

108 Cherry Street, Box 70

Burlington, VT 05402

802-863-7310

www.state.vt.us/health/ems/index.htm

VIRGINIA

Office of Emergency Medical Services

Virginia Department of Health

1538 East Parham Road

Richmond, VA 23228

804-371-3500

www.vdh.state.va.us/oem

WASHINGTON

Office of Emergency Medical and Trauma
   Prevention

Washington Department of Health

PO Box 47853

Olympia, WA 98504-7853

360-705-6700

www.doh.wa.gov/hsqa/emtp

WEST VIRGINIA

Office of Emergency Medical Services

Office of Community and Rural Health
   Services

1411 Virginia Street East

Charleston, WV 25301-3013

304-558-0580

www.wvdhhr.org/ocrhs/ems.htm

WISCONSIN

Bureau of Emergency Medical Services &
   Injury Prevention

Wisconsin Division of Health

PO Box 2659

Madison, WI 53701

608-266-1568

www.dhfs.state.wi.us/dph_emsip/index.htm

WYOMING

Office of Emergency Medical Services and
   Injury Control

Wyoming Department of Health

Hathaway Building, 4th Floor

Cheyenne, WY 82002

307-777-7955

http://wdhfs.state.wy.us/ems

ADDITIONAL INTERNET JOB SITES

http://careers.altavista.com

www.ajb.dni.us

www.bestjobsusa.com

www.careerbuilder.com

www.careermag.com

www.careermosaic.com/cm

www.careerpath.com

www.careers.org

www.emergencyjobs.com/
   intro.htm

www.firecareerassist.com

www.firerecruit.com

www.jobbankusa.com

www.joboptions.com

www.jobvertise.com

www.medctr.ucla.edu

www.psrjobs.com/fireems.htm

www.reidhosp.com

www.123-jobs.com

INDUSTRY-SPECIFIC RECRUITERS

HCRecruiters.com
PO Box 7341
Hicksville, NY 11802
516-735-3765
www.hcrecruiters.com

Innovative Medical Recruiting, LLC
Dale Busbee, President
PO Box 432
Meraux, LA 70075-0432
504-281-0117
www.innomedical.com

Northern Medical Recruiters
17397 Aspen Road
Shafer, MN 55074
651-213-0563
www.ppservice.com/nmr.html

Southern Medical Recruiters
15225 Leeward Dr., #A1
Corpus Christi, TX 78418
800-531-3104
http://southernmed.com

Western Medical Recruiters
PMB605
9121 Atlanta Avenue
Huntington Beach, CA 92646
877-775-2750
http://western-med.com

INTERNATIONAL PARAMEDIC EMPLOYERS

AAC International
PO Box 24077
Dubai
United Arab Emirates
www.aac-dubai.com
9714-314-488
Fax: 9714-311-443
E-mail: aacrecr@emirates.net.ae

Acadian Ambulance and Air Med Services
PO Box 98000
Lafayette, LA 70509-8000
800-259-3333
www.acadian.com
E-mail: eboustany@acadian.com or
        aasi@acadian.com

AEA International/International SOS
331 North Bridge Road
Odeon Towers, 17th Floor
Singapore 0718
65-338-2311
Fax: 65-338-7611
www.aeaintl.com
E-mail: hr.intl@aeaintl.com

Arabian Careers Limited
Berkeley Square House, 7th Floor
Berkeley Square, London W1X 5LB
United Kingdom
011-44-20-7495-3285
Fax: 011-44-20-7681-2901
www.arabiancareers.com
E-mail: recruiter@arabiancareers.com

Atlantic Offshore Medical Services, Ltd.
Victoria Hall
4 Henry Street
St. John's, Newfoundland A1C 6E7
Canada
709-722-4074
Fax: 709-722-6801
www.aoms.nf.net
E-mail: coshea@nfld.com

Environmental Technology of America
   (ENTECH)
2101 Jefferson Street
Lafayette, LA 70501
318-237-3471
Fax: 318-235-6278
www.entech-inc.com
E-mail: entech@iamerica.net

Global Industries
PO Box 442
Sulphur, LA 70664
337-583-5000
Fax: 337-583-5100
www.globalind.com

HCCA International
Washington Square, Suite 311
222 Second Avenue North
Nashville, TN 37201
615-255-7187
Fax: 615-255-7093
www.hccaintl.com
E-mail: usa@hccaintl.com

Helen Ziegler and Associates, Inc.
180 Dundas Street West, Suite 2403
Toronto, Ontario M5G 1Z8
Canada
800-387-4616, 416-977-6914
Fax: 416-977-6128
www.hziegler.com
E-mail: karenf@hziegler.com

Heston (Middle East), Ltd.
Group Head Office
Norton House
Farrants Way
Castletown, Isle of Man IM9 1NR
United Kingdom
44-1624-824595
Fax: 44-1624-825657
www.heston.net
E-mail: jmatthews@heston.net

Holmes and Narver
999 Town and Country Road
Orange, CA 92668
714-567-2400
Fax: 714-543-0955
www.hninc.com
E-mail: coperp@hninc.com

Hurricane Hydrocarbons, Ltd.
300 Fifth Avenue SW, Suite 3100
Calgary, Alberta T2P 3C4
Canada
403-221-8453
Fax: 403-221-8425
www.hurricane-hhl.com

KAMA Enterprises, Inc.
11 SW Fifth Avenue, Suite 2050
Portland, OR 97204-3687
800-433-7791, 503-222-6652
Fax: 503-222-5858
www.kamaenterprises.com

Rainbow Industries S.A.
Rainbow Corporate Centre
44-46 Tomis Boulevard, Suite 30-33
Constantza 8700
Romania
40-41-618-531
Fax: 40-41-619-408
E-mail: itexrom.rainbow@impromex.ro

Raytheon Polar Services Company
61 Inverness Drive East, Suite 300
Englewood, CO 80112
303-790-8606
Fax: 303-790-9130
www.rpsc.raytheon.com
E-mail: resume@polar.org

Triune International
3016 Nineteenth Street NE, Suite 200
Calgary, Alberta, T2E 6Y9
Canada
403-216-3340
Fax: 403-216-3343
E-mail: gordf@telusplanet.net

Ward Industrial Safety
PO Box 185
Cochrane, Alberta T0L 0W0
Canada
800-563-5869, 403-932-7490
Fax: 403-932-4639
www.cadvision.com/ward1st
E-mail: wardpres@hotmail.com

HUMANITARIAN ORGANIZATIONS THAT EMPLOY PARAMEDICS OR PROVIDE VOLUNTEER OPPORTUNITIES

Albert Schweitzer Institute for the
   Humanities
PO Box 550
Wallingford, CT 06492
203-697-2744
Fax: 203-697-3943
www.schweitzerinstitute.org/asi/Mindex.htm
E-mail: info@schweitzerinstitute.org

Cape Cares
Volunteer Coordinator
PO Box 895
West Falmouth, MA 02574-0895
508-394-2419
Fax: 508-548-9701

Care USA
Human Resources
151 Ellis Street NE
Atlanta, GA 30303-2439
404-681-2552
Fax: 404-577-4515
www.care.org

Conservative Baptist International
1501 West Mineral Avenue
Littleton, CO 80120
720-283-2000
Fax: 720-283-9383
www.cbi.org
E-mail: cbi@cbi.org

Florida Association of Voluntary Agencies for
    Caribbean Action
1311 Executive Center Drive, Suite 202
Tallahassee, FL 32301-5029
850-877-4705
Fax: 850-942-5798
www.favaca.org
E-mail: favaca@worldnet.att.net

Guinea Development Foundation, Inc.
140 West End Avenue, Suite 17G
New York, NY 10023
212-874-2911
Fax: 212-496-9549
www.guineadev.com/index.shtml
E-mail: GDF@guineadev.org

Healing the Children, National Headquarters
PO Box 9065
Spokane, WA 99209
509-327-4281
Fax: 509-327-4284
E-mail: national-htc@worldnet.att.net

Helping Hands
948 Pearl Street
Boulder, CO 80302
303-448-1811
Fax: 303-440-7328

Joint Assistance Center
G 17/3 DLF Qutab Enclave, Phase I
Gurgaon
Haryana 122 002
India
0091+124-352141 and 353833
Fax: 0091+124-351308
E-mail: nkjain@jac.unv.ernet.in

Liga International, Inc.
19531 Campus Drive, Suite 20
Santa Ana, CA 92707
949-852-8611
Fax: 949-852-8739
www.liga-flyingdocs.org
E-mail: liga@earthlink.net

Lumiere
209 West Second Avenue
Gastonia, NC 28052
704-868-3703
Fax: 704-868-8991
E-mail: julieKriv@aol.com

Minnesota International Health Volunteers
122 West Franklin Avenue, Suite 110
Minneapolis, MN 55404-2480
612-871-3759
Fax: 612-871-8775

Northwest Medical Teams International, Inc.
PO Box 10
Portland, OR 97207-0010
503-624-1046
Fax: 503-624-1001
www.nwmedicalteams.org
E-mail: mail@nwmti.org

Operation Smile
6435 Tidewater Drive
Norfolk, VA 23509
757-321-7645
Fax: 757-321-7660
www.operationsmile.org

Pacific Missionary Aviation
PO Box 517
Pohnpei, FM 96941
Federated States of Micronesia
691-320-2496
Fax: 691-320-2592
www.pmafms.org
E-mail: PMAPohnpei@mail.fm

Project Amazon
PO Box 913
Morton, IL 61550
309-263-2299
Fax: 309-263-2299
E-mail: dove@dpc.net

Rainforest Health Project
PO Box 624
Deer River, MN 56636
800-870-8325
Fax: 218-246-9674
www.rainforesthealth.org
E-mail: rhp@pobox.com

Street Jude Hospital
PO Box 331
Vieux Fort
Saint Lucia
West Indies
758-454-6799, 758-454-6041
Fax: 809-454-6684, 758-454-6684
E-mail: stjudes@candw.lc

Surgical Medical Assistance Relief Teams
   (SMART)
7015 College, No. 132
Overland Park, KS 66211
913-814-3700
Fax: 913-814-3900
E-mail: rxhelpca@ix.netcom.com

Professional Associations, Unions, and Educational Accrediting Agencies

PROFESSIONAL ASSOCIATIONS AND UNIONS

American Academy of Emergency Medicine
611 East Wells Street
Milwaukee, WI 53202
800-884-2236
www.aaem.org

American Ambulance Association
1255 Twenty-Third Street, NW
Washington, DC 20037-1174
202-452-8888
www.the-aaa.org

American Nurses Association
600 Maryland Avenue, SW,
Suite 100 West
Washington, DC 20024
800-274-4ANA
www.nursingworld.org

Association of Air Medical Services
110 North Royal Street, Suite 307
Alexandria, VA 22314-3234
703-836-8732
www.aams.org

Association of Public Safety
    Communications Officials
2040 South Ridgewood Avenue
South Daytona, FL 32119-8437
888-APCO-911, 904-322-2500
www.apco911.org

Basic Trauma Life Support International, Inc.
1 South 280 Summit Avenue, Court B-2
Oakbrook Terrace, IL 60181
800-495-BTLS
www.btls.org

International Association of Fire Fighters
    (IAFF)
1750 New York Avenue, NW
Washington, DC 20006
202-737-8484
www.iaff.org

Mountain Rescue Association
710 Tenth Street, Suite 105
Golden, CO 80401
503-658-6942
www.mra.org

National Association of Air Medical
 Communication Specialists
PO Box 3804
Cary, NC 27519-3804
877-396-2227
www.naacs.org

National Association of Emergency Medical
 Technicians (NAEMT)
408 Monroe Street
Clinton, MS 39056-4210
800-34-NAEMT
www.naemt.org

National Association of EMS Educators
700 North Bell Avenue, Suite 260
Carnegie, PA 15106
412-429-9550
www.naemse.org

National Association of EMS Physicians
PO Box 15945-281
Lenexa, KS 66285-5945
800-228-3677
www.naemsp.org/sw/index2.html

National EMS Pilots Association
110 North Royal Street, Suite 307
Alexandria, VA 22314-3234
703-836-8930
www.nemspa.org

National Association of EMS Quality
 Professionals
3717 South Conway Road
Orlando, FL 32812-7607
407-281-7396
www.naemsqp.org

National Association of Female Paramedics
1703 Paradise Drive
Kissimmee, FL 34741
407-932-2839
www.nafp.org/

National Association for Search and Rescue
 (NASAR)
4500 Southgate Place, Suite 100
Chantilly, VA 20151-1714
703-222-6277
www.nasar.org/contact.shtml

National Collegiate EMS Foundation
PO BOX 133122
Atlanta, GA 30333-3122
208-728-7342
www.ncemsf.org

National EMS Pilot's Association
110 N. Royal Street, Suite 307
Alexandria, VA 22314
703-836-8930
www.nemspa.org

National Flight Paramedics Association
383 F Street
Salt Lake City, UT 84103
800-381-NFPA
www.nfpa.rotor.com

National Institute for Urban Search and
    Rescue
PO Box 91648
Santa Barbara, CA 93190
805-569-5066
http://niusr.org

National League for Nursing
61 Broadway
New York, NY 10006
800-669-1656, 212-363-5555
www.nln.org

National Registry of Emergency Medical
    Technicians (NREMT)
6610 Busch Boulevard
PO Box 29233
Columbus, OH 43229
614-888-4484
www.nremt.org

National Search and Rescue School
    USCG Training Center
Yorktown, VA 23690-5000
757-856-2273
www2.acc.af.mil/afrccl/nss/index.html

National Ski Patrol
133 South Van Gordon Street, Suite 100
Lakewood, CO 80228
303-988-1111
www.nsp.org

North American EMS Employee
    Organizations Network
c/o Local 2507 DC 37 AFSCME
299 Broadway, Suite 309
New York, NY 10007
212-385-1152
www.neon.org

Society for Academic Emergency Medicine
901 North Washington Avenue
Lansing, MI 48906-5137
517-485-5484
www.saem.org

United States Lifesaving Association
PO Box 366
Huntington Beach, CA 92648
732-775-6449
www.usla.org

EDUCATIONAL ACCREDITING AGENCIES
National

Accrediting Bureau of Health Education
    Schools
803 West Broad Street, Suite 730
Falls Church, VA 22046
703-533-2082
www.abhes.org

Accrediting Commission for Career Schools
    and Colleges of Technology
2101 Wilson Boulevard, Suite 302
Arlington, VA 22201
703-247-4212
www.accsct.org

Accrediting Council for Independent
   Colleges and Schools
750 First Street, NE, Suite 980
Washington, DC 20002-4241
202-336-6780
www.acics.org

Commission on Accreditation of Allied
   Health Education Programs
35 East Wacker Drive, Suite 1970
Chicago, IL 60601-2208
312-553-9355
www.caahep.org

Distance Education and Training Council
1601 18th Street, NW
Washington, D.C. 20009-2529
202-234-5100
www.detc.org

Regional

Middle States

Middle States Association of Colleges and
Schools
Commission on Institutions of Higher
Education
3624 Market Street
Philadelphia, PA 19104
215-662-5606
www.msache.org

New England States

New England Association of Schools and
   Colleges
Commission on Institutions of Higher
   Education
209 Burlington Road
Bedford, MA 01730-1433
781-271-0022
www.neasc.org/cihe/cihe.htm

New England Association of Schools and
   Colleges
Commission on Vocational, Technical, and
   Career Institutions
209 Burlington Road
Bedford, MA 01730-1433
781-271-0022
www.neasc.org/ctci/ctci.htm

North Central States

North Central Association of Schools and
   Colleges
Commission on Institutions of Higher
   Education
30 North LaSalle Street, Suite 2400
Chicago, IL 60602-2504
800-621-7440
www.ncacihe.org

Northwest States

Northwest Association of Schools and
Colleges
Commission on Colleges
1910 University Drive
Boise, ID 83725-1060
208-426-5727
www2.idbsu.edu/nasc

Southern States

Southern Association of Colleges and
Schools
Commission on Colleges
1866 Southern Lane
Decatur, GA 30033
404-679-4500
www.sacscoc.org

Western States

Western Association of Schools and
Colleges
Accrediting Commission for Community and
Junior Colleges
3402 Mendocino Avenue
Santa Rosa, CA 95403
707-569-9177
www.accjc.org

Western Association of Schools and
Colleges
Accrediting Commission for Senior Colleges
and Universities
985 Atlantic Avenue, Suite 100
Alameda, CA 94501
510-748-9001
www.wascweb.org/senior/wascsr.html

APPENDIX C

ADDITIONAL RESOURCES

COLLEGE GUIDES

The College Board College Handbook 2001. (New York: The College Board, 2000).

Peterson's 2 Year Colleges 2001. (Princeton, NJ: Peterson's, 2000).

Vocational & Technical Schools Set 2000. 2 volumes. (Princeton, NJ: Peterson's, 1999).

CAREER-RELATED

Beatty, Richard H. *The Perfect Cover Letter*, 2nd ed. (New York: John Wiley & Sons, 1997).

Great Resume. (New York: LearningExpress, 2000).

Great Interview. (New York: LearningExpress, 2000).

Occupational Outlook Handbook, 2000-2001 ed. (U.S. Bureau of Labor Statistics, Biannual). Available online at www.bls.gov/ocohome.htm

Pohly, Pam. *Directory of Healthcare Recruiters.* (Hays, KA: Pam Pohly Associates, 2000). See website for ordering information: www.pohly.com/dir4.html

FINANCIAL AID AND SCHOLARSHIPS
(Books and Websites)

Books

Cassidy, David J. *The Scholarship Book: The Complete Guide to Private-Sector Scholarships, Fellowships, Grants, and Loans for the Undergraduate* (Upper Saddle River, NJ: Prentice Hall, 2000).

The Complete Scholarship Book (Skokie, IL: SourceBooks/Fastweb.com, 2000).

Peterson's Scholarships, Grants, and Prizes 2001. (Lawrenceville, NJ: Peterson's, 2000).

Websites

FastWeb!—"Helping Over 7 Million Students Find Scholarships, Colleges and Jobs!"
www.fastweb.com
FinAid! The SmartStudent Guide to Financial Aid
www.finaid.org
GrantsNet—source for information on science and medical education
www.grantsnet.org
Student Loan Finance Association
www.slfaloan.com
U.S. Department of Education Federal Student Financial Aid Homepage
www.ed.gov/offices/OSFAP/Students
U.S. Government Programs Benefiting Students (listing)
www.fedmoney.org
Yahoo! Financial Aid page
http://dir.yahoo.com/Education/Financial_Aid

MISCELLANEOUS

Books

Canning, Peter. *Paramedic: On the Front Lines of Medicine.* (New York: Ivy Books, 1998).

Dillman. *EMS Medication Pocket Guide.* (Sudbury, MA: Jones & Bartlett Publishers, 2000).

Hopson, Judi Light. *Burnout to Balance: EMS Stress.* (New York: Prentice Hall, 2000).

Lloyd, Joan E., and Edwin B. Herman. *EMT: Race for Life.* (New York: Ivy Books, 1998).

Miller, Charly D. *Jems EMS Pocket Guide.* (Orlando, FL: Mosby-Year Books, 1996).

Peitzman, Andrew B., et al., eds. *The Trauma Manual.* (Baltimore: Lippincott Williams & Wilkins Publishers, 1998).

Tilton, Buck. *The Wilderness First Responder.* (Old Saybrook, CT: Globe Pequot Press, 1998).

Periodicals

EMS Magazine
Summer Communications, Inc.
7626 Densmore Avenue
Van Nuys, CA 91406-2042
818-786-4367
www.emsmagazine.com

Fire & Rescue Magazine
Kennedy Communications
8 The Old Yarn Mills
Sherborne, Dorset DT9 3RQ
England
44 1935 816030
www.fireandrescue.net

Journal of Emergency Medical Services
JEMS Communications
PO Box 2789
Carlsbad, CA 92018
760-431-9797
www.jems.com

National Fire & Rescue Magazine
3000 Highwoods Boulevard, Suite 300
Raleigh, NC 27604-1029
919-872-5040
www.nfrmag.com

Websites

About.com EMS Webring Guide
*http://firefighting.about.com/careers/firefighting/library/blwebrings.htm?rnk=
r5&terms=EMS*

Emergency Medical Service for Children Initiative
www.ems-c.org

Emergency Services Database
www.district.north-van.bc.ca/admin/depart/fire/ffsearch/mainmenu.cfm

EMS & Emergency Services Links
www.cyberhighway.net/~larsonw/emslinks.htm

EMS Village
www.emsvillage.com

Fire & EMS Information Network
www.fire-ems.net

JEMS 2000 Resource Directory
www.jems.com/ResourceGuide/JEMSResource2000/index.html

MedicCity
www.medic-city.com

Paramedicine.com
www.paramedicine.com

Paramedic Network News (PNN), 210 Taylor Avenue, Selkirk, MB R1A
1G5, Canada
www.paramedic-network-news.com

Port Jefferson Volunteer Ambulance
www.pjvac.org/emslinks.html

Yahoo! Emergency Services
http://dir.yahoo.com/Health/Emergency_Services

STUDYING AND TEST PREP

EMT-Basic Exam (New York: LearningExpress, 2001).
Paramedic Exam (New York: LearningExpress, 2001).
Reasoning Skills Success (New York: LearningExpress, 1998).
The Secrets of Taking Any Test (New York: LearningExpress, 2000).
501 Challenging Logic & Reasoning Problems (New York: LearningExpress,
   1999).
501 Reading Comprehension Questions (New York: LearningExpress, 1999).

Directory of EMT Training Programs

IN THIS appendix, you will find a directory of schools that offer EMT training programs listed by state and alphabetized within each state by city. There are hundreds of vocational, technical, military, and university institutions that offer EMT-Basic and Intermediate certificates and Paramedic associates degrees in cities across the country.

All programs provide school name, address, and phone number, so you can contact each school directly to get more information and application forms for the programs that interest you. This listing is intended to help you begin your search for an appropriate school. The specific schools included in this listing, however, are not endorsed or recommended by LearningExpress. Always contact the schools you are considering to get current information on program requirements and areas of specialization before you apply.

ALABAMA

Lurleen B Wallace State Jr. College
PO Box 1418, Hwy 84 East
Andalusia, AL 36420
334-222-6591
http://lbw.edu

Bessemer State Technical College
PO Box 308
Bessemer, AL 35021
205-428-6391
http://bessemertech.com

University of Alabama at Birmingham
1530 3rd Avenue South
UAB MJH 107 2010
Birmingham, AL 35294
205-934-4011
www.uab.edu

John C. Calhoun State Community College
PO Box 2216
Decatur, AL 35609-2216
256-306-2500
www.calhoun.cc.al.us

George Corley Wallace State Community
 College-Dothan
Route 6, Box 62
Dothan, AL 36303
334-983-3521
http://wccs.cc.al.us

Gadsen State Community College
PO Box 227
Gadsen, AL 35902-0227
256-549-8210
www.gadsenst.cc.al.us

Wallace State Community College-Hanceville
801 Main Street Northwest
PO Box 2000
Hanceville, AL 35077-2000
256-352-8128
www.wallacestatehanceville.edu

University of Alabama at Huntsville
301 Sparkman Drive
Huntsville, AL 35l899
256-824-6290
www.uah.edu

Community College of the Air Force
Maxwell Air Force Base
AL 36112-6613
334-953-6436
www.au.af.mil

Bishop State Community College
351 North Broad Street
Mobile, AL 36603-5898
334-690-6801
www.bscc.cc.al.us

University of South Alabama
182 Administration Building
Office of Admissions
Mobile, AL 36688-0022
334-460-6141
www.southalabama.edu

Trenholm State Technical College
1225 Air Base Blvd.
Montgomery, AL 36108
334-832-9000
website in progress

Northwest Shoals Community College
PO Box 2545
Muscle Shoals, AL 35662
205-381-2813
http://nwscc.cc.al.us

Bevill State Community College
Sumiton Campus
PO Box 800, Hwy 78
Sumiton, AL 35148
205-648-3271
www.bevilst.cc.al.us

Shelton State Community College
1301 15th Street East
Tuscaloosa, AL 35404
205-759-1541 or 205-391-3774
www.shelton.cc.al.us or
    www.alabamafirecollege.cc.al.us

ALASKA
Alaska Vocational Technical Center
809 Second Avenue
Seward, AK 99664-0889
907-224-3322
www.eed.state.ak.us/avtec

ARIZONA
Central Arizona College
8470 North Overfield Road
Coolidge, AZ 85228
520-426-4260
www.cac.cc.az.us

Glendale Community College
6000 West Olive Avenue
Glendale, AZ 85302-3090
623-845-3000
www.gc.maricopa.edu

Mohave Community College
1971 Jagerson Avenue
Kingman, AZ 86401-1299
520-757-0847
www2.mohave.cc.ac.us/mcchome.html

Mesa Community College
1833 West Southern Avenue
Mesa, AZ 85202-4866
480-461-7000 or 480-461-6260
www.mc.maricopa.edu

Phoenix College
1202 West Thomas Road
Phoenix, AZ 85013-4234
602-285-7500
www.pc.maricopa.edu

Scottsdale Community College
9000 East Chaparral Road
Scottsdale, AZ 85256-2626
480-423-6100
www.sc.maricopa.edu

Pima Community College
2202 West Anklam Road
Tucson, AZ 85709-0001
520-206-7000
www.pima.edu

Arizona Western College
9500 S. Avenue 8E
Yuma, AZ 85365
520-317-6000
www.awc.cc.az.us

ARKANSAS
Northwest Arkansas Community College
One College Drive
Bentonville, AR 71712
501-636-9222
http://nwacc.net

South Arkansas Community College
300 South West Ave.
El Dorado, AR 71730
870-864-7195 or 800-955-2289
www.southark.cc.ar.us

Crowley's Ridge Technical School
1620 Newcastle Road
Forrest City, AR 71336
501-633-5411
www.crti.tec.ar.us

East Arkansas Community College
1700 Newcastle Road
Forrest City, AR 71335
870-633-4480
www.eacc.cc.ar.us

Westark Community College
5210 Grand Avenue
PO Box 3649
Fort Smith, AR 71913-3649
501-788-7000

North Arkansas Community Technical College
1515 Pioneer Drive
Harrison, AR 71601
870-391-3250 or 870-743-3000
http://pioneer.nactc.cc.ar.us

Garland County Community College
101 College Drive
Hot Springs, AR 71913
501-760-4222
www.gccc.cc.ar.us or
     www.educationtogo.com/garland

University of Arkansas for Medical Sciences
4301 West Markham, Slot 619
Little Rock, AR 71205
501-686-5730
www.uams.edu

Arkansas Valley Technical Institute
PO Box 506, Hwy 23 North
Ozark, AR 71949
501-667-2117
website in progress

Southeast Arkansas Technical College
1900 Hazel Street
Pine Bluff, AR 71603
870-543-5900
www.seark.org

CALIFORNIA
Bakersfield College
1801 Panarama Drive
Bakersfield, CA 93305-1299
661-395-4301
www.bc.cc.ca.us

Barstow College
2700 Barstow Road
Barstow, CA 92311
760-252-2411
www.barstow.cc.ca.us

Palo Verde College
811 West Chanslor Way
Blythe, CA 92225-1118
760-922-6168
www.paloverde.cc.ca.us

Southwestern College
900 Otay Lakes Road
Chula Vista, CA 91910
619-421-6700
www.swc.cc.ca.us

Columbia College
11600 Columbia College Drive
Sonora, CA 95370
209-588-5100
www.columbiayosemite.cc.ca.us or
  gocolumbia.org

Orange Coast College
2701 Fairview Road
Costa Mesa, CA 92626
714-432-5773
www.orangecoastcollege.com

Glendale Community College
1500 North Verdugo Road
Glendale, CA 91208-2894
818-240-1000
www.glendale.cc.ca.us

Chabot College
25555 Hesperian Boulevard
Hayward, CA 94545-5001
510-723-6700
www.clpccd.cc.ca.us

Imperial Valley College
380 East Aten Road
PO Box 158
Highway 111 and Aten Road
Imperial, CA 92251-0158
760-352-8320
www.imperial.cc.ca.us

Center for Prehospital Care
UCLA-Daniel Freeman Paramedic Education
333 North Prairie Avenue
Inglewood, CA 90301
310-674-7050 ext. 3407
www.cpc.mednet.ucla.edu

Copper Mountain College
PO Box 1398
Joshua Tree, CA 92252
760-366-3791
www.cmccd.cc.ca.us

Antelope Valley College
3041 West Avenue K
Lancaster, CA 93536-5426
661-722-6300
www.avc.edu

Foothill College
12345 El Monte Road
Los Altos Hills, CA 94022-4599
650-949-7777
www.foothill.fhda.edu

NOVA Institute of Health Technology
3000 S. Robertson Boulevard, 3rd floor
Los Angeles, CA 90018
310-840-5777
www.novainstitute.com

Yuba College
2088 North Beale Road
Marysville, CA 95901-7699
530-741-6700
www.yuba.cc.ca.us

Merced College
3600 M Street
Merced, CA 95348-2898
209-384-6190
www.merced.cc.ca.us

North Valley Occupational Center
11450 Sharp Avenue
Mission Hills, CA 91345
818-365-9645
website in progress

Saddle Back College
28000 Marguerite Parkway
Mission Viejo, CA 92692-3635
949-582-4500
www.saddleback.cc.ca.us

Modesto Junior College
435 College Avenue
Modesto, CA 95350-5800
209-575-6362
www.gomjc.org or
    http://mjc.yosemite.cc.ca.us

Monterey Peninsula College
980 Fremont Street
Monterey, CA 93940-4799
831-646-4006
www.mpc.edu

East Los Angeles College
1301 Avenida Cesar Chavez
Monterey Park, CA 91754-6001
323-265-8650
www.elac.cc.ca.us

Napa Valley College
2277 Napa-Vallejo Highway
Napa, CA 94558
707-253-3000 or 800-826-1077
www.nvc.cc.ca.us

Merritt College
12500 Campus Drive
Oakland, CA 94619-3196
510-436-2444 or 510-531-4911
www.merritt.edu

Butte Community College
3536 Butte Campus Drive
Oroville, CA 95965-8399
530-895-2511
www.cin.butte.cc.ca.us

Pacoima Skills Center-Lausd
13545 Van Nuys Boulevard
Pacoima, CA 91331
818-896-9558
www.lausc.k12.ca.us

Pasadena City College
1570 East Colorado Boulevard
Pasadena, CA 91106
626-585-7123
www.paccd.cc.ca.us

Los Medanos College
2700 East Leland Road
Pittsburg, CA 94565-5197
925-439-2182
www.losmedanos.net

Porterville College
100 East College Avenue
Porterville, CA 93257
559-791-2200
www.pc.cc.ca.us

Shasta College
PO Box 496006
Redding, CA 96049-6006
530-225-4769
www.shastacollege.edu

Cerro Coso Community College
College Heights Boulevard
Ridgecrest, CA 93555-9571
888-537-6932
www.cc.cc.ca.us

Riverside Community College
4800 Magnolia Avenue
Riverside, CA 92506
909-222-8000
www.rccd.cc.ca.us

Sierra College
Admissions Office
5000 Rocklin Road
Rocklin, CA 95677-3397
916-781-0430
www.sierra.cc.ca.us

Cosumnes River College
8401 Center Parkway
Sacramento, CA 95823-5799
916-691-7451
www.crc.losrios.cc.ca.us

Skyline College
3300 College Drive
San Bruno, CA 94066-1698
650-738-4100
http://skylinecollege.net

San Diego Miramar College
10440 Black Mountain Road
San Diego, CA 92126-2999
858-536-7800
www.miramarcollege.net

Cuesta College
PO Box 8106
San Luis Obispo, CA 93403-8106
805-546-3100
www.cuesta.cc.ca.us

Palomar Community College
1140 West Mission Road
San Marcos, CA 92069-1487
760-744-1150
www.palomar.edu

College of San Mateo
1700 West Hillsdale Boulevard
San Mateo, CA 94402-3784
650-574-6161
www.gocsm.net

Contra Costa College
2600 Mission Bell Drive
San Pablo, CA 94806-3195
510-235-7800
www.contracosta.cc.ca.us

Santa Ana College
1530 West 17th Street
Santa Ana, CA 92706
714-564-6000
www.sacollege.org

Santa Barbara City College
721 Cliff Drive
Santa Barbara, CA 93109-2394
805-965-0581
www.sbcc.cc.ca.us

Mission College
3000 Mission College Boulevard
Santa Clara, CA 95054-1897
408-988-2200
www.mvmccd.cc.ca.us/mc

College of the Canyons
26455 Rockwell Canyon Road
Santa Clarita, CA 91355
661-259-7800
www.coc.cc.ca.us

Allan Hancock College
800 South College Drive
Santa Maria, CA 93454-6399
805-922-6966
www.hancock.cc.ca.us

Santa Rosa Junior College
1501 Mendocino Avenue
Santa Rosa, CA 95401-4395
707-527-4011 or 800-564-SRJC
www.santarosa.edu

Simi Valley Adult School
3192 Los Angeles Avenue
Simi Valley, CA 93065
805-579-6200
www.simi.tec.ca.us

Lake Tahoe Community College
One College Drive
South Lake Tahoe, CA 96150-4524
530-541-4660
www.ltcc.cc.ca.us

San Joaquin Delta Community College
5151 Pacific Avenue
Stockton, CA 95207-6370
209-954-5151
www2.sjdccd.cc.ca.us or deltacollege.org

Lassen Community College
PO Box 3000
Susanville, CA 96130
530-257-6181
www.lassen.cc.ca.us

Mendocino College
PO Box 3000
Ukiah, CA 95482
707-468-3102
www.mendocino.cc.ca.us

Victor Valley College
18422 Bear Valley Road
Victorville, CA 92392-5849
760-245-4271
www.vvconline.com

College of the Sequoias
915 South Mooney Boulevard
Visalia, CA 93277-2234
559-730-3700
www.sequoias.cc.ca.us

Mount San Antonio College
1100 North Grand Avenue
Walnut, CA 91789
909-594-5611
www.mpsac.edu

College of the Siskiyous
800 College Avenue
Weed, CA 96094
530-938-5215
www.siskiyous.edu

NOVA Institute of Health Technology
Whittier Campus
12449 Putnam Street
Whittier, CA 90602
562-945-9191
www.novainstitute.com

Rio Hondo College
3600 Workman Mill Road
Whittier, CA 90601
562-692-0921
www.rh.cc.ca.us

Los Angeles Harbor College
1111 Figueroa Place
Wilmington, CA 90744
310-522-8214
www.lahc.cc.ca.us

Crafton Hills College
11711 Sand Canyon Road
Yucaipa, CA 92399
909-389-3372
www.sbccd.cc.ca.us/chc/index.htm

COLORADO

San Juan Basin Area Vocational School
PO Box 970
Cortez, CO 81321-9121
970-565-8475
www.sanjuanbasintechschool.org

Morgan Community College
17800 Road 20
Fort Morgan, CO 80701
970-542-3100 or 800-622-0216
www.mcc.cc.coes.edu

Colorado Mountain College
Central Administration & Admissions Office
831 Grand Avenue
PO Box 10001
Glenwood Springs, CO 81602
970-945-8691 or 800-621-8559
www.coloradomtn.edu

Aims Community College
PO Box 69
Greeley, CO 80632-0069
970-330-8008 ext. 6421
www.aims.edu

Lamar Community College
2401 South Main Street
Lamar, CO 81052-3999
719-336-2248
www.lcc.cccoes.edu

Arapaho Community College
2500 West College Drive
PO Box 9002
Littleton, CO 80160
303-797-5620
www.arapahoe.edu

Northeastern Junior College
100 College Drive
Sterling, CO 80751
970-522-6600
www.nejc.cc.co.us

CONNECTICUT

Capital Community Technical College
61 Woodland Street
Hartford, CT 06105
860-520-7800
http://ccc.commnet.edu

Norwalk State Technical College
188 Richards Avenue
Norwalk, CT 06854-1655
203-857-7060
www.ncc.commnet.edu

Three Rivers Community College
Mahan Drive
Norwich, CT 06360
860-892-5756
www.trcc.commnet.edu

Naugatuck Valley Community Technical
    College
750 Chase Parkway
Waterbury, CT 06708-3000
203-575-0328
www.nvcc.commnet.edu

DELAWARE

Delaware Technical & Community College
Owens Campus
PO Box 610
Georgetown, DE 19947
302-856-5400
www.dtcc.edu

DISTRICT OF COLUMBIA

The George Washington University
School of Medicine & Health Science
2300 Eye Street Northwest
Washington, DC 20037
202-994-1000
www.gwumc.edu

FLORIDA

South Florida Community College
600 West College Drive
Avon Park, FL 33825
863-453-6661
www.sfcc.cc.fl.us

Manatee Technical Institute
5603 34th Street West
Bradenton, FL 34210
941-751-7900 ext. 1355

Brevard Community College
1519 Clear Lake Road
Cocoa, FL 32922-6597
321-632-1111
www.brevard.cc.fl.us

Pasco-Hernando Community College
36727 Blanton Road
Dade City, FL 33525-7599
352-567-6701 ext. 3285
www.pasco-hernandocc.com

Daytona Beach Community College
1200 W. International Speedway Boulevard
Daytona Beach, FL 32120
904-254-4426
www.dbcc.cc.fl.us

Lake County Area Vocational-Technical
    Center
2001 Kurt Street
Eustis, FL 32726
352-742-6486

Broward Community College
225 East Las Olas Boulevard
Fort Lauderdale, FL 33301-2298
954-761-7464
www.broward.cc.fl.us

Edison Community College
8099 College Parkway Southwest
Fort Meyers, FL 33906-6210
941-489-9361
www.edison.edu

Indian River Community College
3209 Virginia Avenue
Fort Pierce, FL 34981
561-462-4740
www.ircc.cc.fl.us

Santa Fe Community College
3000 Northwest 83rd Street
Gainesville, FL 32606
352-395-5000
www.santafe.cc.fl.us

Florida Community College at Jacksonville
501 West State Street
Jacksonville, FL 32202
904-646-2300
www.fccj.cc.fl.us

Lake City Community College
Route 19, Box 1030
Lake City, FL 32025
904-752-1396
www.lakecity.cc.fl.us

Palm Beach Community College
4200 Congress Avenue
Lake Worth, FL 33461-4796
561-357-1371
www.pbcc.cc.fl.us

Lake-Sumter Community College
Leesburg Campus
9501 U.S. Highway 441
Leesburg, FL 34788-8751
352-787-3747
www.lscc.cc.fl.us

North Florida Community College
1000 Turner Davis Drive
Madison, FL 32340
850-973-1600
www.nflcc.cc.fl.us

Miami Dade Community College
950 NW 20th Street
Miami, FL 33127
305-237-4337
www.mdcc.edu

American College of Prehospital Medicine
7552 Navarre Parkway
Suite 1
Navarre, FL 32566-7312
800-735-ACPM

Central Florida Community College
PO Box 1388
Ocala, FL 34478-1388
352-237-2111
www.cfcc.cc.fl.us

Valencia Community College
1800 South Kirkman Road
Orlando, FL 32811
407-299-5000
www.valencia.cc.fl.us

St. Johns River Community College
5001 St. Johns Avenue
Palatka, FL 32177-3807
904-312-4200
www.sjrcc.fl.us

Gulf Coast Community College
5230 West Highway 98
Panama City, FL 32401-1058
850-769-1551
www.gc.cc.cc.fl.us

Pensacola Junior College
Warrington Campus
5555 West Highway 98
Pensacola, FL 32507
850-484-1000
www.pjc.cc.fl.us

St. Petersburg Junior College
PO Box 13489
St. Petersburg, FL 33733-3489
727-341-3239
www.spjc.edu

Seminole Community College
Highway 17-92
Sanford, FL 32773-6199
407-328-2025
www.sss.-fl.com

Sarasota County Technical Institute
4748 Beneva Road
Sarasota, FL 34233
941-924-1365
www.careerscape.org

Tallahassee Community College
444 Appleyard Drive
Tallahassee, FL 32304
850-201-6200
www.tallahassee.cc.fl.us

Hillsborough Community College
PO Box, FL 31127
Tampa, FL 33631
813-253-7004
www.hcc.cc.fl.us

Polk Community College
999 Avenue "H" NE
Winter Haven, FL 33881-4299
863-297-1009
www.polk.cc.fl.us

GEORGIA

Darton College
2400 Gillionville Road
Albany, GA 31707
229-430-6740
www.dartnet.peachnet.edu

Augusta Technical Institute
3200 Augusta Tech Drive
Augusta, GA 30906
706-771-4028
www.augusta.tec.ga.us

Carroll Technical Institute

West Central Technical College

997 South Highway 16

Carrollton, GA 30116

770-836-6805

www.carroll.tec.ga.us

DeKalb Technical College

495 North Indian Creek

Clarkston, GA 30021-2397

404-297-9522

www.dekalbtech.org

Dalton State College

Practical Nursing

213 North College Drive

Dalton, GA 30720

706-272-2648

www.daltonstate.edu

Gwinnett Technical Institute

5150 Sugarloaf Parkway

Lawrenceville, GA 30043

770-962-7580

www.gwinnett-tech.org

Lanier Technical Institute

2990 Landrum Education Drive

Oakwood, GA 30566

770-531-6300

www.lanier.tec.ga.us

Valdosta Technical Institute

4089 Val Tech Road

PO Box 928

Valdosta, GA 31603-0928

912-333-2100

www.valdosta.tech.ga.us

Waycross College

2001 South Georgia Parkway

Waycross, GA 31503

912-285-6133

www.way.peachnet.edu

IDAHO

Ricks College

186 Administration Building

Rexburg, ID 83460-1615

208-356-2011

www.ricks.edu

ILLINOIS

Belleville Area College

2500 Carlyle Avenue

Belleville, IL 62221-5899

618-235-2700

www.southwestern.cc.il.us

John A Logan College

700 Logan College Road

Carterville, IL 62918

618-985-3741

www.jal.cc.il.us

City Colleges of Chicago
Chicago City-Wide College
226 West Jackson Boulevard
Chicago, IL 60606
773-265-5343
www.ccc.edu

City College of Chicago
Harold Washington College
30 East Lake Street
Chicago, IL 60601
312-553-5600
www.ccc.edu/hwashington

City College of Chicago, Malcolm X
1900 West Van Buren Street
Chicago, IL 60612-3145
312-850-7125
www.ccc.edu/malcolmx.htm

Loyola University
2160 South 1st Avenue
Building 110
Maywood, IL 60153
708-216-9000
www.luhs.org

McHenry County College
8900 U.S. Highway 14
Crystal Lake, IL 60012-2761
815-455-3700
www.mchenry.cc.il.us

Illinois Central College
One College Drive
East Peoria, IL 61635-0001
309-694-5235
www.icc.cc.il.us

College of DuPage
425 22nd Street
Glen Ellyn, IL 60137
630-858-2800
www.cod.edu

Southeastern Illinois College
3575 College Road
Harrisburg, IL 62946
618-252-6376
www.sic.cc.il.us

Rend Lake College
468 North Ken Gray Parkway
Ina, IL 62846
618-437-5321
www.rlc.cc.il.us

Kankakee Community College
PO Box 888
River Road
Kankakee, IL 60901
815-933-0345
www.kcc.cc.il.us

Frontier Community College
2 Frontier Drive
Fairfield, IL 62837-2601
618-842-3711
www.iecc.cc.il.us

Moraine Valley Community College
10900 South 88th Avenue
Palos Hills, IL 60465-0937
708-974-4300
www.moraine.cc.il.us

South Suburban College
15800 South State Street
South Holland, IL 60473
708-596-2000
www.ssc.cc.il.us

INDIANA

Indiana University Bloomington
300 North Jordan Avenue
Bloomington, IN 47405
812-855-0661 or 812-855-3627
www.indiana.edu

Ivy Tech State College-Southwest
3501 First Avenue
Evansville, IN 47710
812-426-2865
www.ivy.tec.in.us

Lutheran College of Health Professions
3024 Fairfield Avenue
Fort Wayne, IN 46807-1697
219-434-3279

Indiana University-Purdue University
 Indianapolis
425 University Boulevard
Cavenaugh Hall 129
Indianapolis, IN 46202
317-274-4591
www.iupy.edu

Ivy Tech State College-Kokomo
1815 Morgan Street
Kokomo, IN 46903-1373
765-459-0561
www.ivytec.in.us

IOWA

Des Moines Area Community College
Ankeny Campus
2006 South Ankeny Boulevard
Ankeny, IA 50021
800-362-2127
www.dmacc.cc.ia.us

North Iowa Area Community College
500 College Drive
Mason City, IA 50401
515-423-1264 or 888-GO-NIACC
www.niacc.cc.ia.us

Hawkeye Community College
1501 East Orange Road
PO Box 8015
Waterloo, IA 50704-8015
319-296-2320
www.hawkeye.cc.ia.us

Southeastern Community College, North
  Campus
1015 South Gear Avenue
West Burlington, IA 52655-0605
319-752-2731 or 800-828-7322
www.secc.cc.ia.us

KANSAS

Cowle County Community and
  Vocational-Tech School
PO Box 1147
125 South Second
Arkansas City, KS 67005-2662
316-441-5312
www.cowlecollege.com

Neosho County Community College
800 West 14th Street
Chanute, KS 66720
316-431-6222
www.neosho.cc.ks.us

Coffeyville Community College
400 West 11th
Coffeyville, KS 67337-5063
316-251-7700 or 800-782-4732
www.ccc.cc.ks.us

Colby Community College
1255 South Range
Colby, KS 67701
785-462-3984
www.colby.cc.ks.us

Cloud County Community College
2221 Campus Drive
PO Box 1002
Concordia, KS 66901
785-243-1435 or 800-729-5101
www.cloudccc.cc.ks.us

Fort Scott Community College
2108 South Horton
Fort Scott, KS 66701
316-223-2700
www.ftscott.cc.ks.us

Barton County Community College
245 NE 30th Road
Great Bend, KS 67530-9283
316-792-2701 or 316-792-2812
www.barton.cc.ks.us

Highland Community College
606 West Main
PO Box 68
Highland, KS 66035-4165
785-442-6000
www.highland.cc.ks.us

Independence Community College
College Avenue and Brockside Drive
Independence, KS 67301
316-331-4100
www.indy.cc.ks.us

Allen County Community College
1801 North Cottonwood
Iola, KS 66749
316-365-5116
www.allen.cc.ks.us

Kansas City Kansas Community College
7250 State Avenue
Kansas City, KS 66112
913-334-1100
www.kckcc.cc.ks.us

Johnson County Community College
12345 College Boulevard
Overland Park, KS 66210
913-469-8500
www.jccc.net

Pratt Community College
348 Northeast State Road 61
Pratt, KS 67124
316-672-5641
www.pcc.cc.ks.us

KENTUCKY
Eastern Kentucky University
521 Lancaster Avenue
Richmond, KY 40475
859-622-1000
www.eku.edu

LOUISIANA
Louisiana Technical College
Alexandria Campus
4311 South MacArthur Drive
Alexandria, LA 71307-5698
318-487-5439

Our Lady of the Lake College
5345 Brittany Drive
Baton Rouge, LA 70808
225-768-1700
www.ololcollege.edu

Bossier Parish Community College
2719 Airline Drive
Bossier City, LA 71111
318-746-9851
www.bpcc.cc.la.us

Elaine P. Nunez Community College
3710 Paris Road
Chalmette, LA 70043-1249
504-680-2440
www.nunez.cc.la.us

Louisiana Technical College
Avoyelles Campus
PO Box 307, Highway 107
Cottonport, LA 71327
318-876-2701

Louisiana Technical College
Hammond Area Campus
PO Box 489
Hammond, LA 70404
504-549-5063

Louisiana Technical College
Morgan Smith Campus
PO Box 1327
Jennings, LA 70546
337-824-4811

Louisiana Technical College
Sowela Campus
PO Box 16950
3820 Legion Street
Lake Charles, LA 70616-6950
337-491-2688
www.sowela.tec.la.us

University of Louisiana at Lafayette
PO Box 44652
East University Avenue
Layfayette, LA 70504
337-482-1000
www.louisiana.edu

Delgado Community College
615 City Park Avenue
New Orleans, LA 70119-4399
504-483-4004
www.dcc.edu

Louisiana Technical College
Northeast Louisiana Campus
1710 Warren Street
Winnsboro, LA 71295
318-435-2163

MAINE
Kennebec Valley Technical College
92 Western Avenue
Fairfield, ME 04937
207-453-5000
www.kvtc.net

MARYLAND
Anne Arundel Community College
101 College Parkway
Arnold, MD 21012-1895
410-647-7100
www.aacc.cc.md.us

Baltimore City Community College
2901 Liberty Heights Avenue
Baltimore, MD 21215
410-462-8000
www.bccc.state.md.us

The Community College of Baltimore County
CCBC Essex Campus
7201 Rossville Boulevard
Baltimore, MD 21237
410-682-6000
www.ccbc.cc.md.us

University of Maryland Baltimore County
1000 Hill Top Circle
Baltimore, MD 21250
410-455-2291
www.umbc.edu

MASSACHUSETTS
Springfield College
263 Alden Street
Springfield, MA 01109
413-748-3136
www.spfldcol.edu

Massachusetts Bay Community College
50 Oakland Street
Wellesley Hills, MA 02481
781-239-3000
www.mbcc.mass.edu

Quinsigamond Community College
670 West Boylston Street
Worcester, MA 01606-2092
508-853-2300
www.qcc.mass.edu

MICHIGAN
Oakland Community College
Auburn Hills Campus
2900 Featherstone Road
Auburn Hills, MI 48326-2845
248-232-4100
www.occ.cc.mi.us

Kellogg Community College
450 North Avenue
Battle Creek, MI 49017
616-965-3931
www.kellogg.cc.mi.us

Lake Michigan College
2755 East Napier Avenue
Benton Harbor, MI 49022-1899
616-927-3571
www.lmc.cc.mi.us or www.cis-net.net/dmack/

Henry Ford Community College
5101 Evergreen Road
Dearborn, MI 48128
313-845-9600 or 800-585-4322
www.henryford.cc.mi.us

Wayne County Community College
801 West Fort Street
Detroit, MI 48226
313-496-2600
www.wccc.edu

Baker College of Flint
1050 West Bristol Road
Flint, MI 48507
800-964-4299 or 810-766-4000
www.baker.edu

Davenport University
415 East Fulton
Grand Rapids, MI 49503
616-451-3511
www.davenport.edu

Kalamazoo Valley Community College
Texas Township Campus
6767 West "O" Avenue
PO Box, MI 4070
Kalamazoo, MI 49003-4070
616-372-5000
www.kvcc.edu

Lansing Community College
PO Box, MI 40010
Lansing, MI 48901
517-483-1957
www.lansing.cc.mi.us

Muskegon Community College
221 South Quarterline Road
Muskegon, MI 49442
231-773-9131
www.muskegon.cc.mi.us

Great Lakes Jr. College of Business
320 South Washington Avenue
Saginaw, MI 48607-1158
517-755-3457

West Shore Community College
3000 North Stiles Road
PO Box 277
Scottville, MI 49454-9716
231-845-6211
www.westshore.cc.mi.us

Montcalm Community College
2800 College Drive
Sidney, MI 48885
517-328-1250
www.montcalm.cc.mi.us/degree/applied/
    emt.htm

Macomb Community College
14500 East 12 Mile Road
Warren, MI 48093
810-445-7999
www.macomb.cc.mi.us

Emergency Education, Inc.
38140 Executive Drive North
Westland, MI 48185-1972
734-326-0920
www.teameei.com

MINNESOTA

Northeast Metro Technical College
3300 Century Avenue North
White Bear Lake, MN 55110
651-415-5518
www.mneta.org/~nemetro/stw/sectc.html

Ridgewater College
PO Box 1097
2101 15th Avenue NW
Willmar, MN 56201
800-722-1151
www.ridgewater.mnscu.edu

MISSISSIPPI

Jones County Junior College
900 South Court Street
Ellisville, MS 39437
601-477-4025
www.jcjc.cc.ms.us

Itawamba Community College
602 West Hill Street
Fulton, MS 38843
662-862-8000
www.icc.cc.ms.us

Mississippi Gulf Coast Community College
Jefferson Davis Campus
2226 Switzer Road
Gulfport, MS 39507
228-896-2500
www.mgccc.cc.ms.us

University of Mississippi Medical Center
2500 North State Street
Jackson, MS 39216
601-984-1085
www.umsmed.edu

West Harrison County Occupational
Training Center
Long Beach Industrial Park
21500 "B" Street
Long Beach, MS 39560
228-868-6057
www.mgccc.cc.ms.us

Meridian Community College
910 Highway 19 North
Meridan, MS 39307
601-484-8622
www.mcc.cc.ms.us

Hinds Community College
1750 Chadwick Drive
Jackson, MS 39204
601-372-6507
www.hinds.cc.ms.us

Northwest Mississippi Community College
510 North Panola Street
Senatobia, MS 38668
662-562-3200
www.nwcc.cc.ms.us

Southwest Mississippi Community College
College Drive
Summit, MS 39666
601-276-2000
www.smcc.cc.ms.us or
    www.ssemt@smcc.cc.ms.us

MISSOURI

Cape Girardeau Area Vocational-Technical
    School
301 North Clark Avenue
Cape Girardeau, MO 63701
573-334-0826

Jefferson College
1000 Viking Drive
Hillsboro, MO 63050-2441
636-789-3951
www.jeffco.edu

Penn Valley Community College
3201 Southwest Trafficway
Kansas City, MO 64111
816-759-4000
www.kemetro.cc.mo.us

St. Louis Community College at Meramec
11333 Big Ram Boulevard
Kirkwood, MO 63122
314-984-7608
www.stlcc.cc.mo.us

Crowder College
601 Laclede Street
Neosho, MO 64850-9160
417-451-3223
www.crowder.cc.mo.us or
    www.crowdercollege.net

Rolla Area Vocational-Technical School
1304 East Tenth Street
Rolla, MO 65401
314-573-3726

St. Louis Community College at Florissant
    Valley
3400 Pershall Road
St. Louis, MO 63135-1499
314-595-4200
www.stlcc.cc.mo.us

St. Louis Community College
    at Forest Park
5600 Oakland Avenue
St. Louis, MO 63110-1393
314-644-9100 or 314-644-9111
www.stlcc.cc.mo.us/fp

St. Louis University
2500 Abbott Place
St. Louis, MO 63143
314-977-2500
www.abbott-ihm.org

Sikeston Area Vocational Technical School
1002 Virginia
Sikeston, MO 63801
573-471-5440

North Central Missouri College
1301 Main Street
Trenton, MO 64683
660-359-3948
www.ncmc.cc.mo.us

East Central College
PO Box 529
Union, MO 63084-0529
636-583-5195
www.ecc.cc.mo.us

MONTANA

Montana State University Great Falls
College of Technology
2100 16th Avenue South
PO Box 6010
Great Falls, MT 59406
800-446-2698
www.msugf.edu

NEBRASKA

Mid-Plains Technical Community College
Interstate 20 and Highway 83
North Platte, NE 69101-9491
308-532-8740
www.mpcc.ne.us

Creighton University
2500 California Plaza
Omaha, NE 68178
800-282-5835
www.creighton.edu

Western Nebraska Community College
1601 East 27th Street
Scottsbluff, NE 69361
308-635-6010
www.wncc.net

NEVADA

Community College of Southern Nevada
   Cheyenne Campus
3200 East Cheyenne Avenue
North Las Vegas, NV 89030
702-651-4000
www.ccsn.nevada.edu

NEW HAMPSHIRE

New Hampshire Technical Institute
11 Institute Drive
Concord, NH 03301-7412
603-271-7134 or 800-247-0179
www.nhti.net

NEW JERSEY

Camden County College
PO Box 200
Blackwood, NJ 08012-0200
856-227-7200
www.camdencc.edu

Union County College
1033 Springfield Avenue
Cranford, NJ 07016-1528
908-709-7000
www.ucc.edu

Atlantic Community College
J Building Admissions
5100 Black Horse Pike
Mays Landing, NJ 08330
609-343-4922 or 609-823-5766
www.atlantic.edu

Essex County College
303 University Avenue
Newark, NJ 07102-1798
973-877-3000
www.essex.edu

University of Medicine and Dentistry of New
   Jersey
School of Health Related Professions
65 Bergen Street
University Heights
Newark, NJ 07107-3001
973-972-5000
www.umdnj.edu/homeweb/index.htm

Bergen Community College
400 Paramus Road
Paramus, NJ 07652
201-447-7100
www.bergen.cc.nj.us

Passaic County Community College
One College Boulevard
Paterson, NJ 07505-1179
973-684-6868
www.pccc.cc.nj.us

Essex County College
West Essex Campus
730 Bloomfield Avenue
West Caldwell, NJ 07006
973-403-2560
www.essex.edu/WestEssex

NEW MEXICO
University of New Mexico
2700 Yale Boulevard SE
Albuquerque, NM 87106
505-277-2446 or 505-272-5757
www.hsc.unm.edu/som/emermed/emsacad

New Mexico Junior College
5317 Lovington Highway
Hobbs, NM 88240-9123
800-657-6260
www.nmjc.cc.nm.us

Dona Ana Branch Community College
MSC 3DA, PO Box 30001
Las Cruces, NM 88003-8001
505-527-7500
http://dabcc-www.nmsu.edu

Eastern New Mexico University-Roswell
PO Box 6000
Roswell, NM 88202
505-624-7000
www.roswell.enmu.edu

NEW YORK
Broome Community College
Upper Front Street
PO Box, NY 1017
Binghamton, NY 13902-1017
607-778-5000
www.sunybroome.edu

Corning Community College
One Academic Drive
Corning, NY 14830
607-962-9221
www.corning-cc.edu

Fiorello H. LaGuardia Community College of
CUNY
31-10 Thomson Avenue
Long Island City, NY 11101-3071
718-482-7206

Borough of Manhattan Community College
of CUNY
199 Chambers Street
Room 5300
New York, NY 10007
212-346-8101
www.bmcc.cuny.edu

Erie Community College-South Campus
4041 Southwestern Boulevard
Orchard Park, NY 14127-2199
716-851-1003
www.ecc.edu

Monroe Community College
Public Safety Training Center
Damon City Campus
228 E. Main Street
Rochester, NY 14604
716-262-1467
www.monroe.edu

Schenectady County Community College
78 Washington Avenue
Schenectady, NY 12305-2294
518-381-1366
www.sunyccc.edu

Rockland Community College
145 College Road
Suffern, NY 10901-3699
914-574-4237
www.sunyrockland.edu

Hudson Valley Community College
80 Vandenburgh Avenue
Troy, NY 12180
518-629-HVCC or 877-325-HVCC
www.hvcc.edu

Erie Community College-North Campus
6205 Main Street
Williamsville, NY 14221
716-851-1797
www.ecc.edu

NORTH CAROLINA

Asheville-Buncomb Tech Community
College
340 Victoria Road
Asheville, NC 28801
828-254-1921
www.asheville.cc.nc.us

Western Carolina University
Cullowhee, NC 28723
828-227-7211
www.wcv.edu

Gaston College
201 Highway 321 South
Dallas, NC 28034
704-922-6214
www.gastoncollege.org

Catawba Valley Community College
2550 Highway 70 Southeast
Hickory, NC 28602
828-327-7009
www.cvcc.cc.nc.us

Coastal Carolina Community College
444 Western Boulevard
Jacksonville, NC 28546-6877
910-938-6294
www.coastalcarolina.org

Guilford Technical Community College
PO Box 309
Jamestown, NC 27282-0309
336-334-4822 ext. 5350
http://technet.gtcc.cc.nc.us

Wake Tech Community College
9101 Fayetteville Road
Raleigh, NC 27603
919-662-3500
www.wake.tec.nc.us

Montgomery Community College
PO Box 787
Troy, NC 27371
910-576-6222
www.mcc.montgomery.cc.nc.us

Wilson Technical Community College
PO Box 4305
Wilson, NC 27893-3310
252-291-1195
www.wilsontech.cc.nc.us

NORTH DAKOTA

Med Center One EMS Education
PO Box 5525
Bismarck, ND 58505
701-224-6075

OHIO

University of Cincinnati
Raymond Walters College
9555 Plainfield Road
Cincinnati, OH 45236
513-745-5700 or 513-558-4995
www.rwc.uc.edu

Cuyahoga Community College
Metropolitan Campus
2900 Community College Avenue
Cleveland, OH 44115
216-987-4030
www.tri-c.cc.oh.us

Columbus State Community College
550 East Spring Street
Columbus, OH 43215
614-227-2400
www.cscc.edu

Sinclair Community College
444 West Third Street
Dayton, OH 45402-1460
937-512-2500
www.sinclair.edu

Butler County JVS District-D
Rusell Lee Career Center
3603 Hamilton Middletown Road
Hamilton, OH 45011
513-868-6300
www.butlercountyjvs.com

Cuyahoga Community College-Eastern
Campus
4250 Richmond Road
Highland Hills, OH 44122
216-987-2000
www.tri-c.cc.oh.us

Lakeland Community College
7700 Clocktower Drive
Kirtland, OH 44094
440-953-7100
www.lakeland.cc.oh.us

Lima Technical College
4240 Campus Drive
Lima, OH 45804
419-221-1112
www.ltc.tec.oh.us

Ehove Career Center
316 West Mason Road
Milan, OH 44846
419-499-4663 ext. 280
www.ehove-jvs.k12.oh.us

Tri-Rivers Career Center
2222 Marion-Mount Gilead Road
Marion, OH 43302
740-389-6347
www.tririvers.com

Hocking Technical College
3301 Hocking Parkway
Nelsonville, OH 45764-9588
740-753-3591
www.hocking.edu

Belmont Technical College
120 Fox-Shannon Place
St. Clairsville, OH 43950
740-695-9500
www.belmont.cc.oh.us

Clark State Community College
PO Box 570
570 East Leffel Lane
Springfield, OH 45501
937-328-6027
www.clark.cc.oh.us

Jefferson Community College
4000 Sunset Boulevard
Steubenville, OH 43952-3598
740-264-5591 or 800-68-COLLEGE
www.jeffersoncc.org

University of Toledo
2081 West Bancroft
Toledo, OH 43606-3390
419-530-4242
www.utoledo.edu

Youngstown State University
One University Plaza
Youngstown, OH 44555
330-742-3000 or 877-468-6978
www.ysu.edu

OKLAHOMA

Rogers State College
1701 West Will Rogers
Claremore, OK 74017
918-343-7546
www.rsu.edu

Redlands Community College
1300 South Country Club Road
El Reno, OK 73036
405-262-2552
www.redlands.cc.ok.us

Oklahoma Christian University of Science
and Arts
PO Box 11000
East Memorial Road
Oklahoma City, OK 73136-1100
405-425-5050
www.oc.edu

Oklahoma City Community College
7777 South May Avenue
Oklahoma City, OK 73159-4444
405-682-1611
www.okc.cc.ok.us

OREGON

Southwestern Oregon Community College
1988 Newmark Avenue
Coos Bay, OR 97420-2912
800-962-2838
www.southwestern.cc.or.us

Clackamas Community College
19600 South Molalla Avenue
Oregon City, OR 97045
503-657-6958
www.clackamas.cc.or.us

Oregon Health Science University
3181 Southwest Sam Jackson Park Road
Portland, OR 97201
503-494-7800
www.ohsu.edu

Portland Community College
1200 SW 49th Avenue
PO Box 19000
Portland, OR 97280-0990
503-977-4519
www.pcc.edu

Umpqua Community College
1140 College Road
PO Box 967
Roseburg, OR 97470
541-440-4600
www.umpqua.cc.or.us

Chemeketa Community College
4000 Lancaster Drive NE
Salem, OR 97309-7070
503-399-5000
www.chemek.cc.or.us

PENNSYLVANIA

Northhampton County Area Community
  College
3835 Green Pond Road
Bethlehem, PA 18020-7599
610-861-5500
www.northhampton.edu

Harrisburg Area Community College
One HACC Drive
Harrisburg, PA 17110-2999
717-780-2300 or 800-ABC-HACC
www.hacc.edu

Luzerne County Community College
1333 South Prospect Street
Nanticoke, PA 18634-3899
570-740-0200 or 570-740-0300
www.luzerne.edu

MCP Hahnemann University
245 North 15th Street
M.S. 472
Philadelphia, PA 19102-1192
215-762-4293
www.mcphu.edu

Community College of Allegheny County,
  Allegheny Campus
800 Allegheny Avenue
Pittsburgh, PA 15233
412-237-3100
www.ccac.edu

PUERTO RICO

Universal Technology College of Puerto Rico
111 Comercio Street
Aguadilla, PR 00605
809-882-2065

Center de Estudios Multidisciplinarios
602 Barbosa Avenue
Hato Rey, PR 00917
809-765-4210

Inter American University of Puerto Rico
Metropolitan Campus
PO Box 1293
Hato Rey, PR 00919
809-250-1912 or 809-765-1270
www.metro.inter.edu

Inter American University of Puerto Rico
Main Campus
PO Box 5100
San German, PR 00683
787-892-3090
http://coqui.metro.inter.edu/academic.html

Electronic Data Proessing College of
Puerto Rico, Inc.
555 Munoz Rivera Avenue
San Juan, PR 00919
809-765-3560

SOUTH CAROLINA

Greenville Technical College

PO Box 5616

Greenville, SC 29606-5616

864-250-8111

www.greenvilletech.com

TENNESSEE

Northeast State Technical Community
    College

2425 Highway 75

PO Box 246

Blountville, TN 37617-0246

423-323-3191 or 423-282-0800

www.nstcc.cc.tn.us

Chattanooga State Technical Community
    College

4501 Amnicola Highway

Chattanooga, TN 37406-1018

423-697-4400

www.cstcc.cc.tn.us

Columbia State Community College

PO Box 1315

Columbia, TN 38402-1315

931-540-2722

www.coscc.cc.tn.us

Volunteer State Community College

1480 Nashville Pike

Gallatin, TN 37066

888-335-8722

www.vscc.cc.tn.us

Roane State Community College

276 Patton Lane

Harriman, TN 37748

423-882-4599 or 423-882-4610

www.rscc.tn.us

Jackson State Community College

2046 North Parkway

Jackson, TN 38301

901-424-3520

www.jscc.cc.tn.us

Southwest Tennessee Community College

PO Box 780

Memphis, TN 38101-0780

901-333-STCC or 877-717-STCC

www.stcc.cc.tn.us

Walters State Community College

500 South Davy Crockett Parkway

Morristown, TN 37813

423-318-2763

www.wscc.cc.tn.us

TEXAS

Amarillo College

2201 S. Washington

Amarillo, TX 79109

806-371-5000

www.actx.edu

Trinity Valley Community College

100 Cardinal Drive

Athens, TX 75751

903-677-TVCC (8222)

www.tvcc.cc.tx.us

Austin Community College
5930 Middle Fiskville Road
Austin, TX 78752-4390
512-223-3030
www.austin.cc.tx.us

Lee College
PO Box 818
Baytown, TX 77522
281-427-5611
www.lee.edu

Howard College
1001 Birdwell Lane
Big Spring, TX 79720
915-264-5106
www.howardcollege@hc.cc.tx.us

Frank Phillips College
PO Box 5118
Borger, TX 79008
806-274-5311 ext. 777 or 749
www.fpc.cc.tx.us

The University of Texas at Brownsville and
Texas Southmost College
80 Fort Brown
Brownsville, TX 78520
956-544-8200
www.utb.edu

Blinn College, Bryan Campus
PO Box 6030
Bryan, TX 77805-6030
979-821-0220
www.blinncol.edu

Montgomery College
3200 Highway 242
College Park Drive
Conroe, TX 77384
963-273-7236
www.woodstock.edu

Del Mar College
101 Baldwin Boulevard
Corpus Christi, TX 78404
361-698-1255 or 800-652-3357
www.delmar.edu

El Centro College
Main and Lamar Streets
Dallas, TX 75202-3604
214-860-2037
www.ecc.dcccd.edu

El Paso Community College
PO Box 20500
El Paso, TX 79998
915-831-2000
www.epcc.edu

Tarrant County Junior College
Northeast Campus
828 Harwood Road
Hurst, TX 76054-3299
817-515-6100
www.tccd.net

North Central Texas College
1525 West California Street
Gainesville, TX 76240-4699
940-668-7731
www.nctc.cc.tx.us

Galveston College
4015 Avenue Q
Galveston, TX 77550-7496
409-763-6551
www.gc.edu

San Jacinto College-College North
5800 Uvalde Road
Houston, TX 77049-4599
281-458-4050
www.sjcd.cc.tx.edu

Kilgore College
300 South High
Longview, TX 75601
903-984-8531
www.kilgore.cc.tx.us

Laredo Community College
West End Washington Street
Laredo, TX 78040-4395
956-721-5117
www.laredo.cc.tx.us

North Central Texas College
Lewisville Campus
190 West Main
Lewisville, TX 75057-3978
214-420-0089
www.nctc.cc.tx.us

Texas Tech University
Admissions
Box 45005
Lubbock, TX 79409
806-742-1482 or 806-743-3218
www.texastech.edu

Angelina College
PO Box 1768
Lufkin, TX 75902
936-639-1301
www.angelina.cc.tx.us

Collin County Community College
Central Park Campus
2200 West University Drive
McKinney, TX 75070
972-548-6790
www.cccd.edu

Midland College
3600 North Garfield
Midland, TX 79705-6399
915-685-4500
www.midlands.cc.tx.us

Odessa College
201 West University
Odessa, TX 79764
915-335-6432
www.odessa.edu

San Jacinto College Central
8060 Spencer Highway
PO Box 2007
Pasadena, TX 77501-2007
281-476-1501
www.sjcd.cc.tx.us

San Antonio College
1300 San Pedro
San Antonio, TX 78212
210-733-2000
www.accd.edu/sac/sacman/sac.htm

University of Texas Health Science
Center at San Antonio
7703 Floyd Curl Drive
San Antonio, TX 78229-3900
210-567-2621 or 210-567-7000
www.uthscsa.edu

Texas State Technical College
Sweetwater Campus
300 College Drive
Sweetwater, TX 79556
915-235-7300
www.sweetwater.tstc.edu

Texarkana College
2500 North Robison Road
Texarkana, TX 75599-0001
903-838-4541
www.tc.cc.tx.us

College of the Mainland
1200 Amburn Road
Texas City, TX 77591
409-938-1211
www.collegeofthemainland.com

Tomball College
30555 Tomball Parkway
Tomball, TX 77375
281-351-3300
www.tc.nhmccd.cc.tx.us

Tyler Junior College
PO Box 9020
Tyler, TX 75711-9020
800-687-5680 or 903-510-2200
www.tyler.cc.tx.us

McLennan Community College
1400 College Drive
Waco, TX 76708
254-299-8622
www.mcc.cc.tx.us

Weatherford College, Mineral Wells Campus
225 College Park Drive
Weatherford, TX 76086
817-594-5471 or 800-287-5471
www.wc.edu

UTAH
Bridgerland Applied Technology Center
1301 North 600 West
Logan, UT 84321
435-753-6780
www.batc.tec.ut.us

Weber State University
Admissions Office
1137 University Circle
Ogden, UT 84408-1137
801-626-6743
www.weber.edu

Uintah Basin Applied Technology Center
1100 East Lagoon Street (124-5)
Roosevelt, UT 84066
435-722-4523 or 435-789-4866
www.ubatc.tec.ut.us

Dixie College
225 South 700 East
St. George, UT 84770
435-652-7500
www.dixie.edu

VIRGINIA
Northern Virginia Community College
8333 Little River Turnpike
Annandale, VA 22003-3796
703-323-3000
www.nv.cc.va.us

WASHINGTON
Bellingham Technical College
3028 Lindbergh Avenue
Bellingham, WA 98225
360-738-0221
www.beltc.ctc.edu

Central Washington University
400 East 8th Avenue
Ellensburg, WA 98926
509-963-1211
www.cwu.edu

Lower Columbia College
1600 Maple
PO Box 3010
Longview, WA 98632
360-577-2311
http://lcc.ctc.edu

University of Washington
Medical Technology Building
Box 357110
Seattle, WA 98195
206-543-2100
www.washington.edu

Spokane Community College
1810 North Greene Street
Spokane, WA 99217-5399
509-533-7000 or 800-248-5644
www.scc.spokane.cc.wa.us

Tacoma Community College
6501 South 19th Street
Tacoma, WA 98466-6139
253-566-5000
www.tacoma.ctc.edu

WEST VIRGINIA

West Virginia Northern Community College

Wheeling Campus

1704 Market Street

Wheeling, WV 26003

304-233-5900

www.northern.wvnet.edu

WISCONSIN

Fox Valley Technical College

1825 North Bluemound Drive

Appleton, WI 54912

920-735-5600

www.foxvalleytech.com

Lakeshore Technical College

1290 North Avenue

Cleveland, WI 53015

888-468-6582

www.gotoltc.com

Moraine Park Technical College

235 North National Avenue

PO Box 1940

Fond du Lac, WI 54936-1940

920-922-8611 or 800-472-4554

www.moraine.tec.wi.us

Black Hawk Technical College

6004 Prairie Road

PO Box 5009

Janesville, WI 53547

608-756-4121

www.blackhawk.tec.wi.us

Gateway Technical College

3520 30th Avenue

Kenosha, WI 53144-1690

262-564-2200

www.gateway.tec.wi.us

Western Wisconsin Tech College

304 North 6th Street

LaCrosse, WI 54601

608-785-9571

www.western.tec.wi.us

Madison Area Technical College

3550 Anderson Street

Madison, WI 53704-2599

608-246-6212

www.madison.tec.wi.us

Waukesha County Technical College

800 Main Street

Pewaukee, WI 53072

262-691-5566

www.waukesha.tec.wi.us

Nicolet Area Tech College

PO Box 518

County Highway G

Rhinelander, WI 54501

715-365-4411 or 800-544-3093

www.nicolet.tec.wi.us

North Central Technical College

1000 Campus Drive

Wausau, WI 54401

715-675-3331

www.northcentral.tec.wi.us

WYOMING

Casper College

125 College Drive

Casper, WY 82601

307-268-2110

www.cc.whecn.edu

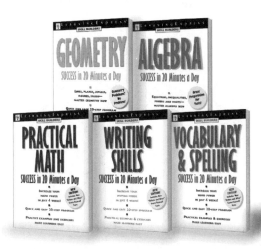

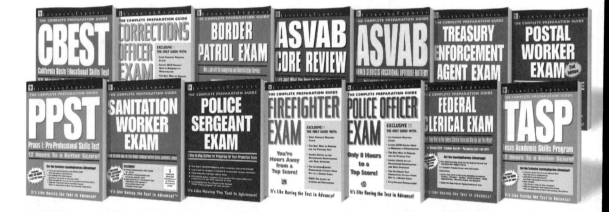